This book belongs to

24

sagithini

I am sit

Best Loved
ANIMAL
Tales for BEDTIME

Best Loved
ANIMAL
Tales for BEDTIME

p

THIS IS A PARRAGON BOOK

This edition published in 2000

Parragon
Queen Street House
4 Queen Street
Bath BA1 1HE

ISBN 0 75253-505-6

Printed in Italy

Stories by Nicola Baxter
Designed by Amanda Hawkes
Text illustrations by Duncan Gutteridge

Contents

The Friendly Pig

Once upon a time, there was a very friendly pig. Now many pigs are friendly in their way. They will nuzzle your legs if you go into their sty, and sometimes they will nibble your trousers, which is rather annoying. But this particular pig, called Pongo, was very friendly to everyone. And this turned out to be rather a problem.

Pongo was given his name by the farmer's daughter, when her father returned from market with him early one morning. "We'll call him Pongo," she giggled, as the new pig was put into his sty, "because pigs are so smelly!"

"They're *not* smelly," protested her father, who had a soft spot for pigs. "It's only that they are sometimes fed smelly food."

"And what comes out the other end of them isn't exactly perfumed," laughed his wife.

"I really don't think," said the poor farmer, going rather pink, "that this is a suitable subject for the breakfast table. Eat up your crispies, Rosie."

But the name of the new pig stuck, and he was Pongo from that day to this.

On the first day, the farmer put Pongo in a beautiful new sty, with lots of straw, a big trough of water and some delicious pig nuts to munch.

Pongo strolled around his new home, which did not take long. He rolled around in the straw for a while, and found it pleasantly scratchy on his back. He had a drink of water, and found it cool and refreshing. He had a quick snack of pig nuts, and found them very tasty. Then he rubbed his back against the wall and looked around.

The sty was certainly spacious. Several pigs could have made a happy home there. But Pongo was not happy. There was something missing. Yes, there was definitely something very important missing.

Now you might think that Pongo had everything a pig could wish for, but you would be wrong. As I mentioned before, Pongo was a friendly pig. He had looked all the way round his sty and there was no doubt in his mind. It didn't contain a friend.

Pongo never was a pig to let the straw settle under his feet. He wiggled his snout at the catch on the gate and found that it might be tricky for a foolish human being to undo, but it was child's play for a pig. In no time at all, he was trotting happily off into the yard to find someone friendly to talk to.

The first animal that Pongo met was a bustling hen.

"Good morning," said the pig politely. "Pongo's the name."

"Henrietta Hen," squawked the feathery fowl. "Pleased to meet you, I'm sure."

Pongo gave a big smile. He had made a friend already.

"And I'm pleased to meet you," he said. "I knew a very nice hen back at my last farm. I'm sure you and I can be great friends."

Maybe so, maybe not," squawked Henrietta, "but just at the moment, I haven't time to stop. I've got six little chicks in a hen coop the size of a shoebox, and it's almost time I laid some more eggs. Where everyone is going to fit in, I don't know."

"May I make a suggestion?" snuffled Pongo. "I've a beautiful sty, far too large for a bachelor pig like myself. There is straw for a nest and a trough of water and even some quite tasty snacks. Why not make yourself at home there? Your family would like it, I'm sure."

Henrietta Hen cocked her head on one side. Live in a pigsty? Well, it was better than a shoebox, she supposed.

"I'm much obliged to you, Pongo," she said briskly. "We'll move in this morning. But I hope you won't mind me mentioning something…"

"Anything, dear lady!"

"Well, you will be careful, won't you, where you put your trotters when my new eggs are laid?"

"Don't give it a moment's thought," said Pongo. "I was winner of the pig polka prize on my last farm two years running. You will find my footwork as dainty as any you have seen."

Pongo wandered happily across the farmyard. Not only had he made a friend, but he had found a whole family to share his sty. What could be more delightful than that?

The next animal that Pongo met was Gobbles the goat. He was tethered by a long chain to one side of the barn. He could reach a trough of food and one of water, but he couldn't reach any of the very beautiful flowers in the garden next to the farmhouse.

"Greetings!" called Pongo. "Allow me to introduce myself. Pongo's the name. Pongo by name but not by nature! Ha ha!"

"My name is Gobbles," said the goat with a giggle. "Gobbles by name *and* by nature, I'm afraid."

"Is that, excuse my mentioning it," said Pongo politely, "the reason for the chain?"

"It is," said Gobbles. "There was an unfortunate incident with some washing. Who would think that humans could be so finicky about their clothes? I mean, why do they need *two* legs in a pair of trousers? They would stay on perfectly well with just one."

"Well, but they do have two legs themselves," said Pongo reasonably. "I know it's very unfortunate for them not to have four legs like us, and perhaps we shouldn't mention it, but you can understand how, having only two legs, they might like to cover them up."

"I suppose so," said the goat. "But did you know that humans are lopsided?"

"Lopsided?"

"Yes, they have to have special boots because their feet are different shapes. Even the two feet they do have are not the same, you see."

"I didn't know that," said Pongo. "How did you find it out?"

"There were four wellington boots standing outside the back door," explained Gobbles, "and I, well, I had a little chew at a couple of them. I thought that would be fine, because no human can wear more than two boots at once, after all. But it seems I nibbled the wrong two boots. The two that were left were for the same foot. Now I'm stuck here at the end of this chain, and I'm not very happy, as you can well imagine."

"Would you promise," said Pongo, "on your honour as a goat, not to eat washing or boots if I undid your chain?"

"I would certainly promise that, and I would be your friend for life," said Gobbles, eyeing the flowers around the farmhouse.

Of course, when he heard that, Pongo didn't hesitate. He wiggled his snout and rattled the chain until it was undone. Then he trotted off happily to make another new friend.

Primrose the cat was lazily sleeping on a sunny wall when Pongo walked by. The pig cleared his throat politely.

"Good morning," he said. "I'm Pongo, and I'm glad to see you enjoying yourself this fine and friendly morning."

The cat rubbed her paws across her eyes. "I'm pleased to meet you," she said. "But it is not a fine morning by any means. The farmer has just told me that he will sell me if I don't catch more mice."

"That's dreadful," said Pongo. "Could I help at all?"

Primrose tried to summon up a picture of a pig catching a mouse, but it seemed very, very unlikely.

"I don't think so," said the cat, jumping down to a bowl of milk

that had been left for her on the
grass below.

"Why does the farmer want
you to catch the mice?" asked
Pongo, curiously.

"Because they eat the corn in
the barn," said Primrose with a

large yawn. "I thought everyone knew that."

"So if we could persuade them to eat something else," asked Pongo, "the farmer would be happier with you?"

"I suppose so," Primrose agreed, "but I don't see how such a thing could be done."

"Just leave it to me," said Pongo. "I'm quite good at talking to mice. There were a lot of them on my last farm."

So Pongo wiggled his snout and undid the latch on the barn. Sure enough, inside there were hundreds of sacks of corn. There were also hundreds of mice!

"Pongo's the name. Could I have a word?" called the friendly pig.

Half an hour later, Pongo and the mice had finished a most satisfactory chat. A few minutes after that, he accompanied the mice to the back of the farmhouse and used his famous snout-wiggling technique to open the pantry window. Then he strolled off back to the farmyard, happy to have made yet more new friends.

On the way, he introduced himself to Horace the horse, who was looking wistfully out of his stable at the lively goings-on in the farmyard.

"I wish *I* could go into your sty," said the horse, although there really would not have been room for him. "I wish I could go anywhere at all, but I just have to stay here all day. I really can't remember the last time one of the children took me for a ride."

"Why not come for a bit of a stroll with me?" asked Pongo. "It's such a friendly farmyard out here."

"But I can't get out," explained Horace sadly.

Pongo had a careful look at the bolts on the stable. "No problem," he said.

The farmer was in a hurry when he rushed in for his lunch,

but as he sat down, one or two odd things that he had only half noticed on his way across the farmyard began to creep into his tired mind.

"There are hens in the pigsty," he said slowly, "and they're eating the pig nuts."

A foolish face smiled at him from the window.

"There's a goat in the flower-bed," cried the farmer, running out of the farmhouse, "and he's eating my petunias!"

He raced across the yard, pulling on his coat as he went.

"There's a horse in the barn, and he's eating my corn!" he

cried, diving back towards the house again.

At the doorway, he collided with his wife.

"There are mice in my pantry, and they're eating my pies!" she shouted, as the force of the collision swept them both into the farmhouse.

"And there's a pig in my parlour, and he's eating my dinner!" The farmer collapsed into a chair.

"Good afternoon," said Pongo. "We didn't have much of a chance for a chat this morning. How are things going this very fine day?"

You may not be surprised to learn that Pongo the friendly pig no longer lives on the farm. After quite a lot of muttering about chops and chitterlings, the farmer took him to a children's farm, where Pongo is in his element. All day long, he makes new friends and chats with his neighbours. And the latch on his pen is extra-specially-wiggly-snout-proof!

The
Baby Boom

It was springtime. Wherever you looked on Appletree Farm there were babies.

The big tabby cat that lazed in the sunshine on the roof of the pigsty had four fluffy little kittens.

The sheepdog that spent all year nipping at the heels of the slowest sheep had five lively black and white puppies.

Down on the pond, Daisy Duck swam proudly at the head of ten fluffy little yellow ducklings.

Over at the hen coop, Henrietta Hen had five little chicks, who pecked in the dirt beside her.

Every sheep had a little leaping lamb – and some had

two. Every cow had a calf wobbling along beside her.

Even the farmer's wife, who had been rather tired for the past few months, produced twins, much to the delight of the farmer, who did a jig in the yard in his wellingtons and pyjamas.

Everywhere you looked, there were cuddly little babies and contented, if sleepy, mammas.

Only Horace the horse was feeling unhappy.

"Why haven't I had a baby?" he asked Gobbles the goat.

"Well, Horace," said Gobbles with a giggle, "you can't have a baby, you know. You see, you're a he-horse, not a she-horse."

"So?" said Horace.

"Well, chaps like us don't have babies. That's a job for, you know, *girls*."

"I don't see why," said Horace. "I'd make a very good mother."

"You'd make a lovely mother," Gobbles agreed, "but it just can't be, Horace, and you must stop thinking about it."

But Horace couldn't stop thinking about it. All around him, proud mothers were showing off their babies. And Horace's stable seemed empty and cold.

Horace became sadder and sadder. His old head drooped over his door, as the harrassed mothers and their broods bustled past.

Then, one day, Gobbles overheard Henrietta and Daisy exchanging a few clucks and quacks behind the hen coop.

"I'm rushed off my feet morning, noon and night," said Henrietta. "I don't have a moment to myself. What I wouldn't give for five

minutes to put my feet up, much
as I love my little chicks."

"I know just what you mean,"
replied Daisy. "I'm on the go all
the time, too. On the pond. Off
the pond. Into the reeds. Out of
the reeds. And they're not safe to
be left, oh no. Only yesterday,
the smallest one tried to climb

up a drainpipe. Imagine! I'm so tired, my wings are wobbling."

Gobbles crept away and gave the discussion some thought. Then he hurried along to Horace and leaned casually against the stable door.

"How are you, Horace?" he asked, cheerfully.

"So, so," said Horace, his face looking even longer than usual. "I'm still not a mother, you know."

"I know, Horace," said Gobbles firmly. "We've discussed that, you know. But have you ever considered babysitting?"

"Babysitting?"

"Yes, babysitting."

Horace looked confused. "Sitting on babies? Won't it hurt them?"

"No, no," cried Gobbles. "What a sheltered life you've led, Horace. Babysitting means looking after babies while their parents have a rest or go out for the evening or something. You have to be just as careful as a mother, but only for a little while."

Horace shifted from hoof to hoof. He began to look interested.

"Would anyone *want* me to be a babysitter?" he asked.

"I think they would," said the goat. "And I will help you to write a notice to put behind the barn, where the farmer won't see it."

This is what Gobbles wrote:

Babysitting service offered.

Chicks and ducklings a speciality.

Reliable horse. References available.

Horace read it, swinging his great head. "But I haven't got any references," he said.

"Well, I've written a couple for you," said Gobbles. "One is what the farmer would have written for you if he had had time. It says, 'Horace has taken my children for rides for many years. He has always been very careful and steady. Signed, the Farmer.' The other one is from me. It says, 'When I first came to the farm, I was only a little goat. Horace looked after me until I could take care of myself. I would not hesitate to recommend him. Signed, Gobbles the Goat.' What do you think?"

Horace was touched. He had to clear his throat before speaking.

"That's very decent of you, Gobbles," he said, in a husky voice. "I'll do my best not to let you down."

"I know you will," said Gobbles. "Now, I'll go and pin this up, and you can wait for customers."

There was a flurrying and a scurrying in the farmyard when Horace's notice went up. Before he knew what was happening, the huge horse had a queue stretching from his stable door all the way back to the duck pond. Within half an hour, he was booked solid for a fortnight, and at least two of the sheep had enquired whether he was thinking of offering a full-time nanny service.

So if you should happen to visit Appletree Farm, don't be surprised if you see a large horse with ten little ducklings on his back. And if you peer into

Horace's stable, you are just as likely to see two fluffy lambs playing leaplamb over his head as you are to find five playful puppies pulling at his ears.

As for Horace, he has never been happier.

"I still think I'd be a good mother," he says to Gobbles sometimes.

"Oh, Horace, don't let's go through all that again," says the goat. "After all, you make an absolutely *lovely* aunty."

The
Farmer
Wants a
Wife

Do you know the rhyme about the farmer who wants a wife?

The farmer's in his den,
The farmer's in his den,
Ee eye addy oh!
The farmer's in his den.
The farmer wants a wife,
The farmer wants a wife...

and so it goes on. Well, once there was a farm where the farmer really needed a wife – only he didn't seem to realise it.

In fact, it was the animals who first decided that Farmer William needed someone to live with him and look after him.

"He never looks very happy," said the biggest pig. "Every day he mooches about and hardly sees anyone. That's not healthy for a human being any more than it is for a pig. We've got to do something about it."

"Do you think he's ill?" asked the billy goat. "That can make people look miserable. I've noticed that."

"No," said the shy sheep, in a soft little voice. "I don't think he's ill. I think he's *lonely*, like I was when I had to stay on my own in the meadow last year. I know human beings don't always like to be in big groups like us, but I don't think they should be alone either."

"That's a good point," said the piebald pony. "He often comes and chats to me on his way back to the farmhouse. That's probably because he hasn't anyone else to talk to. You know, what he needs is a wife and a family. I wonder why he hasn't got them?"

"I think it's because he's so busy," quacked the diving duck. "He's working on the farm from morning till night. He never gets a chance to go out and meet someone nice. *We* have lots of free time, after all," and the diving duck looked coyly at the dabbling drake, who had been bringing her special weeds from the pond for a couple of weeks. "But I can't see what we can do about the farmer's free time," the diving duck went on, when the blush had faded from her feathers. "We can't do most of the work on the farm, after all. And it would look pretty strange to the farmer if we did."

The other animals agreed that the diving duck had probably hit upon the farmer's real problem. Each of them went away and had a long think about how to find the farmer a wife. Now some animals think more quickly than others, but this was quite a big problem, so it wasn't until a few weeks later that the animals got together again to talk about how they could help the farmer.

"It seems to me," said the billy goat, "that there's no way we can get the farmer to leave the farm more often. If he's to find a wife, it will have to be someone who comes to the farm. I've made a little list in my head, but I might have forgotten someone."

"Well, there's the post lady," said the piebald pony. "She's quite jolly, and she seems to like coming to the farm. She doesn't worry if her shoes get muddy like that lady delivering the telephone directories did."

"No, that's true," said the diving duck. "The post lady must certainly be on the list. And what about the egg lady?"

Twice a week, a lady in a big van came to collect the eggs from William's Farm. She was usually quite cheerful, too, and she had been heard to admire the big brown eggs that Farmer William's hens laid.

"The egg lady is another very good possibility," agreed the billy goat. "And I was thinking of the lollipop lady."

Just outside the farm entrance was a road crossing, where the lollipop lady helped the school children to cross the road twice a day. Once, when the weather was very cold, Farmer William had helped to tow her car out of a slippery patch beside the road. Ever since then, the lollipop lady had popped in every so often, bringing a fruit cake or an apple pie for the farmer.

"Yes," said the biggest pig. "I think the lollipop lady is the most likely of all, because she seems to like Farmer William a lot. What can we do to help them spend more time together?"

This was something else that needed thinking about. The animals went away for another week or two. Then the biggest pig called a meeting.

"I've had a really good idea," she said. "But it's a bit risky, and it will take some organising."

'What is it?" neighed the piebald pony. "Tell us quickly."

"Well," said the biggest pig, "we all think that the farmer needs to spend more time with one of those ladies, so that he has a chance to see how nice it would be to be married to her. I wondered if we could sort of accidentally on purpose lock them up together in the small barn one day."

At first sight, this seemed a ridiculous idea. How could such a thing be managed, and would it work? The animals were not sure. But when the pig explained what she had in mind, they began to think that it might be the answer to the problem after all.

"The only thing is," said the diving duck, "that I don't think we could do it three times. The farmer would be sure to get suspicious. We'd have to put them all in the barn with the farmer together. I know that's not ideal, but if he has to spend time with all of them at once, it will be easy for the farmer to see which one he likes best."

There was just one morning a week when the plan might work. That was on a Thursday, when the egg lady and the post lady arrived at about the same time, and the lollipop lady would just be getting ready to leave her post outside the farm gates.

On the first Thursday after their meeting, all the animals were ready. Luckily, it was a fine, sunny day, so no one was delayed.

"You know what you have to do?" the biggest pig said to the tiniest pig.

"Yes," squeaked the piglet. "I'm ready, Aunty."

"Wait for my signal," said the biggest pig, as the egg lady drew up and greeted the farmer, who had come out to meet her.

"Wait for it, wait for it…" whispered the biggest pig, as the post lady's van swept into the yard, and she got out.

"Now!" cried the biggest pig.

The tiniest pig ran across the yard as fast as his little legs would carry him, squealing at the top of his voice. Behind him ran the diving duck, quack, quack, quacking. Behind *her* galloped the piebald pony, neighing loudly.

One after the other, the tiniest pig and the diving duck and the piebald pony ran into the barn.

"What the …?" cried the farmer. "Excuse me a moment!" And he ran into the barn to see what was going on.

No sooner did Farmer William skid round the door than the biggest pig ran straight up behind him and knocked him over into a pile of bales. Then, to make quite sure he didn't escape, she sat on him (but quite gently).

"Help!" yelled the farmer. "Help! Somebody help!"

The farmer shouted so loudly that the egg lady, the post lady and even the lollilop lady all ran into the barn to help.

Quick as a flash, the billy goat lowered his head and charged at the barn doors. *Crash! Crash!* They slammed shut, and the dabbling drake flew up to push down the latch. The farmer, the egg lady, the post lady and the lollipop lady were all well and truly trapped in the barn.

Outside, the shy sheep and the billy goat discussed tactics.

"How long do you think we should leave them?" asked the shy sheep. "Would half an hour be long enough, do you think? Or an hour, perhaps?"

"Oh, no," said the goat. "We must leave them several hours at least, only the lollipop lady will have to be out in time to help the children this afternoon."

So the animals sat out in the yard all morning. They would have twiddled their thumbs if they had had thumbs to twiddle. Some of the sillier hens started to try to guess which of the ladies would marry the farmer. The favourite seemed to be the egg lady, because she had been so complimentary about their eggs, but the shy sheep favoured the post lady, and there were several votes for the lollipop lady too.

At last the clock on the church tower struck one, and the billy goat said it was time to undo the barn doors.

The animals could tell right away that the experiment had not been a success. The ladies looked furious and stalked off across the yard as if they couldn't get away fast enough.

When the farmer emerged, he had a face like thunder, and he looked very suspiciously at the latches on the barn door.

The animals had to wait for the biggest pig, who had been shut up with the humans, to tell them what had happened.

"It was a disaster," sighed the biggest pig. "You know, the small barn is not very big."

"Yes, yes," said the other animals eagerly.

"And Farmer William had been cleaning out my sty this morning."

"So what?" asked the animals.

"So the ladies said he was terribly *smelly*!"

"*What*?" cried the animals. "But that's a *lovely* smell!"

"Not to all humans, apparently," said the biggest pig. "I'm afraid Farmer William got rather upset too. He didn't like them saying he was smelly. I suppose you can understand it really."

"So you don't think the post lady, or the egg lady, or the lollipop lady will be Farmer William's wife?"

"No," said the biggest pig. "In fact, I don't think any of them will even talk to him in future. If only I hadn't had that stupid idea. Now we've managed to get rid of all three candidates at once. I'm sorry, friends."

Of course, the other animals told her not to worry at all, but they all secretly vowed not to meddle in the farmer's life again. He was not destined to be married, and that was that. They had tried and failed.

The next day, the biggest pig had a very sore leg. Perhaps it was all the running about she had done the day before. The farmer noticed it when he brought her feed that morning and at once went to telephone the vet.

The vet arrived at midday. She was new to the local practice, but she at once discovered what was wrong with the biggest pig and gave her some medicine to put it right.

"Thank you very much," said Farmer William, opening the vet's car door for her.

Next morning, Farmer William brought the biggest pig her feed as usual. He looked down at her and scratched her back.

"Oh dear," he said. "Oh dear, oh dear, oh dear. I don't like the look of that leg. I'm afraid we'll have to call the vet again."

"Whatever is the matter with him," wondered the biggest pig. "My leg is completely better this morning. I don't need the vet. Anyway, I thought she had very cold hands."

This time it was almost evening before the vet arrived.

"I'm sorry," she said to Farmer William. "I was very busy today."

Farmer William blushed and stepped carefully around a

muddy puddle in the yard.
Normally he would simply have
splashed through in his boots,
but for no reason that the
animals could see, he had
changed his clothes and put on a
smart pair of shoes instead.

"Here she is, poor old girl,"
said the farmer, looking down at
the biggest pig.

The biggest pig started to get
to her feet, anxious to show that
all was well, but she found that
the farmer was resting his knee
none too lightly on her shoulder,
so that it was impossible for her
to stand. Surely the vet would
realise that her leg was better?

But the vet was shaking her head. "Yes, this hasn't cleared up as quickly as I had hoped," she said, opening her bag. "I think I may have to come back again tomorrow to check this. In fact, it may take several visits."

"That's wonderful," said the farmer. "I mean, oh dear, poor old pig."

"Not so much of the old," said the biggest pig to herself, and she grunted to attract the farmer's attention. But Farmer William was busy looking at the vet, and the vet only had eyes for Farmer William. "But I'm the patient!" squealed the biggest pig.

It was amazing how many of the animals on William's Farm were poorly that year. Farmer William spotted problems the animals weren't even aware of. He even asked the vet to check the diving duck's twelve ducklings (for the dabbling drake had courted her most successfully). Soon the animals were fed up with being prodded and poked and bandaged.

"The sooner those two get married, the better," said the billy goat firmly.

And, of course, that's exactly what happened. Now everyone is living happily ever after down on William's Farm.

The
Hen in a
Hurry

There was a flurry of feathers and a pattering of skinny little feet, and Hannah Hen scurried round the corner of the hen coop.

"That hen is always in such a hurry," said Dora Duck. "Where is she going so fast?"

"I don't know," said Gerda Goat. "She never stops still long enough for me to ask her."

All day long, Hannah Hen rushed around, pausing only for a second to peck at the grain the farmer's wife scattered for her or to fluff up her feathers when the wind blew more keenly. Even at night, when all the other animals were sleeping peacefully, she could be heard scratching and scurrying in the hen coop. No one had ever seen her sitting still for a moment.

"It's not natural," said Gerda. "Even hens have to rest some time, and whatever is she going to do when she has eggs to sit on? How will she be able to keep still long enough?"

But Hannah never did have eggs to sit on. She laid one fine brown egg each day for the farmer, but she was quite happy for him to take it away with the other eggs. Then she would scurry off about her business.

Now one problem with the hen's busy ways was that she hardly ever had time to sit and think. In fact, she was not really in the habit of thinking at all, and that was nearly her undoing.

One springtime, a wily old fox came sniffing around the hen coop. He noticed that most of the hens were sitting comfortably in their nests, but Hannah Hen was rushing about as usual. The hens on the nests would be hard to catch, for they were safe inside the hen coop, but Hannah was out and about all day long. The hungry fox licked his lips. He loved a chicken dinner.

Next morning, when Hannah rushed around the side of the old barn, the fox was waiting.

"Where are you off to in such a hurry?" he asked. "It's a beautiful day. Why don't you stop to enjoy it, my dear?"

But the hen did not even pause to think who was talking to her.

"I can't stop," she said. "I've got much too much to do today."

"I'm sorry to have disturbed you," said the fox politely.

Next morning, the young fox was waiting again.

"Still so busy?" he asked, as Hannah scuttled around the building he was leaning against.

"Always busy," puffed Hannah, slightly out of breath. She had a vague impression that she was talking to a reddish kind of dog, and she knew that there were dogs who sometimes liked to chase chickens for fun, but she did not really feel worried.

Next morning, as she scurried on her way, Hannah was in for a surprise. The clever fox had put a big, open bag just round the corner. As Hannah came hurtling along, she ran straight into the bag. The fox quickly pulled the strings around the top of the bag, and Hannah Hen was well and truly trapped inside.

"Help!" cried Hannah. "Help! Help! Help!"

But the thick bag muffled her cries, and the fox had soon carried her far away from the farmyard and all her friends.

I'm sorry to say that the fox had very bad manners. He did not lay the table and sit down nicely for his dinner as his mother had taught him. No, he simply opened the bulging bag, stretched his jaws wide, and swallowed Hannah Hen whole.

Well, that's the end of Hannah Hen, you are saying, but you are wrong. Inside the fox's tummy, Hannah was as busy as ever. She ran up and down and tickled his tonsils. She fluffed out her feathers and kicked his ribs. And her scratchy little feet went scurrying up and down all day long.

The fox very quickly began to regret that he had caught and eaten that lively hen.

"Oooooh!" he groaned. "What is happening in my tummy?" He

could feel those skinny feet marching up and down in his insides, and he began to feel very ill indeed.

Not knowing what to do, the fox crawled off to his mother's den, stopping every now and then for a moan and a groan.

The mother fox took just one look at her son.

"What have you been eating?" she asked. "It certainly is something that should have been left on your plate."

"It was a hoppity hen," said the fox. "I caught her so cleverly, but now she is hopping up and down in my tummy, and it *hurts*."

"I'm not surprised," said his mother. "Did you sit down properly at the table and eat her like a well-brought-up little fox?"

The younger fox hung his head. The answer was plain for his mother to see.

Then his mother went to the cupboard and got out a big packet of white powder. She mixed it with some water and put it in a bowl.

The younger fox looked doubtfully at the mixture. As it sat in its bowl, it fizzled and hissed as though it was alive.

"There is only one thing to do," said the mother fox. "That hen will have to come right out of your tummy. And this mixture is the stuff to do it."

She picked up the bubbly mixture and gave it to her son. But despite the scratchy feet in his tummy, the fox hesitated.

"Go on," cried his mother, her patience now at an end. "You got into this fix in the first place by not listening to your wise old mother. You had better start now."

So the younger fox lifted the bowl and drank the white mixture down with one big gulp.

Inside the fox, the mixture bubbled and rumbled, and you have never seen a fox look so surprised as when Hannah Hen came jumping right out of his mouth. As you can imagine, her fidgety fast feet didn't stop for a moment. She was hurrying over the hill and back to the hen coop as fast as her scrawny little legs would carry her.

Well, Hannah is a changed hen now. She has raised three beautiful broods of fluffy chicks, and she is always careful to peep round corners before she hurries ahead. As for the fox, he has not been seen in the farmyard for many a long year, and I hear that his table manners have improved enormously!

The
Kindly Cow

Once upon a time, there was a cow called Buttercup who could not do enough to help others. If baby animals were shivering in the winter winds, she let them snuggle down with her in the warm straw in the cowshed. If a farm animal was feeling poorly, she would trot happily off to find some fresh green dandelions and daisies to make him feel better. She was a very kindly cow, and it upset her when she wasn't able to help her fellow creatures.

In fact, as the years went by, the cow began to be rather a *worrier*. She didn't wait for animals to come to her with their problems, she tried to foresee difficulties long before they arose.

Patrick Pig was almost driven to distraction by the kindly cow's worries about his health.

"Your sty is very draughty, my friend," she said to him one day. "Won't you let me block up these cracks with some squelchy mud from the yard?"

"No, no," said Patrick Pig. "I like that draught. It keeps me cool in summer, and even in the winter it's nice to have some fresh air. I'm happy with my sty just the way it is, thank you."

But Buttercup could not let the matter alone. She was sure that the sty was not healthy. Every day for the next fortnight she trotted along to see Patrick.

"Was it you I heard coughing last night, Pat?" she asked. "Would you like me to borrow that woolly scarf from the scarecrow? It would help to keep your delicate throat warm."

"My throat isn't delicate," said Patrick. "And it wasn't me coughing last night."

Next day, the cow was back.

"Here is a mouthful of straw from my cowshed," she said. "It will help to keep your trotters off that hard, cold floor. You must take care of yourself in this chilly weather, my friend."

"That's very kind of you, Buttercup," said Patrick, "but I really don't need more straw. I have a lovely big bed in the corner, and I quite like to keep the rest of the floor clear, so that I can practise my tap dancing."

"Tap dancing! Oh, is that really wise?" Now the cow had something new to worry about.

"You're not a *small* pig, Patrick. What about the strain on your knees and ankles, not to mention your trotters? And please be careful that you don't slip."

"That's why I don't want more straw in my sty," explained Patrick patiently, but the kindly cow was now so worried she could hardly think straight.

"Never mind the straw, Patrick," she said anxiously. "I'm going to hurry off to find you some embrocation for your joints. I'm sure I saw the farmer put some away in the barn the other day."

The pig had no idea what embrocation was, but he was pretty sure it was something he didn't want. I'm afraid he trotted off to see his friend the goat, so that he was quite definitely *out* when Buttercup returned.

Of course, the other animals discussed Buttercup and how difficult she was becoming.

"It's such a shame," said the goat. "She always means well, but I find myself going out of my way to avoid her."

"I know what you mean," said Ducky Duck. "Last week she was worried that the water was too cold for my ducklings. She thought they would all catch cold in their little legs. I tried as hard as I could to explain to her that ducklings are *meant* to spend a lot of time in cold water, but she just wouldn't listen. In the end, I'm afraid we had to swim out into the middle of the pond so that she couldn't bother us any more."

As the weeks passed, Buttercup became more and more impossible. But the animals also noticed that she was becoming very tired and miserable herself. One day, Patrick Pig, who had successfully managed to avoid the dreaded embrocation, asked Buttercup whether she was feeling well.

"Oh, I'm fine, Patrick," sighed Buttercup. "Don't worry about me, please."

But her head sagged towards the ground as she spoke.

"No, no, Buttercup," insisted the pig. "You're always so anxious about *us*. Now we're worried about *you*. We can all see that you're not yourself at the moment. Please tell me what's the matter."

Buttercup looked unhappily at the pig. She was always anxious about other animals' problems, but she felt awkward talking about her own.

"It's nothing really," she said. "I'm just being a silly old cow, but the trouble is I'm not getting much sleep at the moment."

"Isn't your lovely cowshed comfortable?" asked Patrick. "It

always looks very cosy, and I have heard some of the younger animals say that it is a fine place to stay."

"Oh, how kind," said Buttercup. "No, it isn't that. My cowshed is perfect. It's just that I have so many anxious thoughts going round and round in my head, I simply can't drift off to sleep."

"What sort of anxious thoughts?" asked Patrick, although he was rather afraid he might regret asking the question.

"Oh, silly things really," said Buttercup. "I worry about whether the baby goats have nibbled the flowerbeds and

made their tummies sore. I get concerned about the sheep and whether they are too hot in their woolly coats when the sun shines. I wonder whether the farmer has remembered to put his winter vest on when the wind is whistling round the farmhouse. I think about the little birds in their nests and get anxious about the farm cat creeping up on them. I worry..."

"Yes, yes, I see!" Patrick Pig felt he had to interrupt before he began to feel as anxious as poor Buttercup did.

"Don't you think, old friend," he suggested gently, "that you could leave the animals and humans concerned to worry about themselves? After all, your worries don't stop bad things happening – or good ones either, for that matter."

"I know you are right, Patrick," sighed the cow. "But those thoughts just buzz round and round in my poor old head, until I am so worried I simply *can't* get to sleep, no matter what I do."

Now Patrick really did feel worried himself, but he was a sensible pig who knew that the best thing to do with worries is to talk them over with someone else. He hurried off once again to discuss the matter with his friend the goat, and while he was there, most of the other animals came along to see what was happening. Soon everyone was trying to think of a way to help the kindly cow.

"Counting sheep is very good," said one little lamb. "That's what my mother says, and she's very clever about that kind of thing. But you do have to be able to count up to quite a high number, and I'm not sure how good cows are at counting."

"Neither am I," said Patrick, "and we don't want to give Buttercup something *else* to worry her, do we?"

"Drinking milk before bedtime is supposed to be very good for helping you to sleep," said Ducky Duck. "I wouldn't fancy it myself, but other animals like milk."

"The problem there is that the only place we can get milk from is Buttercup herself," said the goat. "That doesn't sound very sensible to me. What about exercise? I've heard that a brisk walk in the fresh air can help humans *and* animals to get a good night's sleep."

"But Buttercup gets lots of exercise," said a sensible sheep. "She is always running about to see whether we are all well and happy. I don't think more of that would help her very much."

In the end, the animals had to admit that they really did not know how to help Buttercup. And perhaps that was just as well, because the next night something happened that helped Buttercup to help herself.

The following day was cold and windy, but as the afternoon

wore on, dark storm clouds gathered over the farm. All sensible animals hurried into their cowsheds and hen coops and barns and sties. The ducks and ducklings sheltered deep in the reeds at the edge of the pond, and sheep cuddled together in the shelter of a wall.

As the first heavy drops of rain fell, the wind blew harder. It whistled round the farmyard and rattled the farmhouse windows. It banged gates and upset feed buckets. First wisps of straw danced through the restless air. Then larger objects began to be thrown about by the wind.

At the height of the storm, there came a horrible creaking sound. Louder and louder it grew, until ... *crash!* ... the huge tree that stood in the corner of the farmyard fell with a noise like thunder, just missing the pigsty.

As though it had exhausted itself with the effort of pushing over the tree, the wind suddenly dropped, and the rain stopped. One by one, the animals came cautiously out of their homes and shelters to see what the huge noise had been.

What a mess there was! The farmyard was filled with broken branches and twigs. There were broken tiles from the roof of the barn and, of course, a massive tree lying diagonally across the farmyard. It was a miracle that none of the buildings had been hit by the tree, and it was very, very lucky too that all the animals and the farmer in his farmhouse had not been harmed.

In fact, no one really seemed to have been seriously affected by the storm. At least, that was what all the animals thought until they heard a tiny twittering sound coming from the branches of the fallen tree. A little bird, who had nested in the highest branches, was trapped by a network of broken twigs and was calling for help.

It didn't take the goat two minutes to free the bird, who was not hurt but very frightened.

"Oh, what am I going to do?" she cried. "My home has been destroyed. Thank goodness my nestlings had already flown away to homes of their own."

"There are lots of other trees on the farm," said Patrick Pig.

"What about Home Wood? You could build a new nest there."

But the little bird shuddered and hid her head under her wing. It was kindly Buttercup who understood at once what was wrong.

"Is it that you are afraid now that trees are not very safe, my dear?" she asked.

"Yes, yes," twittered the bird in a tiny voice. "I don't think I could feel happy on a swaying branch any more. How could I sleep, wondering if my home was going to fall with a crash at any moment? Perhaps I could make a nest somewhere else."

"I have the perfect place," smiled Buttercup. "My cowshed is warm and safe. There is plenty of straw to build a nest. I would be delighted if you would come and live there."

"But is there anywhere to perch and sing?" asked the little bird. "Although it would frighten me to stand on a branch now, I would miss not being able to sing whenever I felt happy."

Buttercup looked puzzled, but Patrick gave a happy snuffle and came up with an excellent suggestion for the little bird.

"What about Buttercup's horns?" he asked. "They would

make a lovely perch for you whenever you wanted to sing. I am sure that Buttercup would be careful not to move her head too much while you were sitting and singing there."

It was the perfect solution, and the little bird agreed gratefully. But the strange thing was that Buttercup also benefited from the arrangement.

"You are looking much happier, Buttercup," said Patrick one day soon after the storm.

"Yes," said the kindly cow. "Each evening, the little bird perches on my horns and sings me to sleep. All the worries in

my head go right away when I hear her lovely song, and in the morning, I am fresh and ready to go about my business as usual."

It was true. Having a good night's sleep meant that kind Buttercup could think clearly during the day. She no longer bothered the animals with her own worries about their health and happiness, but she was always ready to help any creature who needed her. As usual, Patrick Pig put it well.

"That storm was frightening at the time," he said, "but now we are all happy. Those stormclouds certainly had silver linings!"

The
Difficult
Duck

What do ducks like to do? Well, they enjoy swimming on ponds, where they can dive and dabble and generally do duck-like things. They quite like foraging in the reeds and weeds at the edge of ponds too, and they are often quite happy to gobble up bread thrown to them by passing humans. Those are the things that ducks like to do, aren't they?

Not when it comes to Daphne Duck, they're not.

Daphne really is the most difficult duck you have ever met. She lives on Five Meadows Farm, where she regularly drives the farmer to distraction. Let me explain what she is like.

Now most farmers, as you know, get up very early in the morning. The little birds that sing the dawn chorus while it is still dark have barely started their practice scales when most farmers are hopping out of bed. But have you ever heard of a *duck* joining the dawn chorus? You've guessed it. Daphne does. At three o'clock in the morning, when even farmers are usually in their beds, Daphne sits on the bathroom windowsill of the farmhouse and begins the loudest quacking you have ever heard.

Every morning, the farmer wakes with a start, for his bedroom is right next to the bathroom, and, I'm afraid, he mutters several rather rude words before he pulls the pillow over his head and tries to get half an hour's sleep. Even through several thousand feathers, it is surprisingly easy to hear the loud quack of Daphne Duck. It is also surprisingly difficult to go back to sleep after being woken by an alarm duck. Somehow that quacking sound seems to echo in his head.

Outside the farmhouse of Five Meadows Farm, there is a

beautiful duck pond. It is fringed with reeds and filled with fish. On the lily pads in the middle, several little green frogs croak and hop. No duck could wish for a finer home.

But will Daphne deign to live on the perfect pond? Oh no. She makes a nuisance of herself waddling round the farmyard, bouncing first into the pig's water trough and then into the horse's. In fact, all the animals are fed up with having Daphne's muddy feet paddling in their water, but it seems impossible to stop her. Even when the pig grunts, and the horse snorts at her, Daphne pays no attention to either of them.

"What's a little mud between friends?" she quacks. "It's lovely, healthy stuff. Everyone should eat a little mud every day."

Of course, Daphne was quite wrong about that, as she was about most things, so I don't want to hear that you have been munching mud, all right?

Most ducks eat pondweed and fish and other watery delicacies. Daphne's diet, of course, was quite different. That duck liked apples. Yes, round, ripe apples were her favourite food, and she didn't mind where she stole them from. The farmer's fruit bowl was often raided, whenever he foolishly forgot to close the kitchen window.

Of course, it is not natural for ducks to eat apples. Their beaks are not built for it. But Daphne seemed to manage very well. She munched the ripe fruits, core and all, and seemed to thrive on them. Indeed, no other duck had such glossy plumage.

I expect you are wondering why the farmer bothered to keep this troublesome bird. More than once, his wife found her eyes straying through the duck recipes in her largest cookery book. And the farmer often dreamed he could smell the delicious aroma of *duck à l'orange* – especially at three o'clock in the morning.

But in their heart of hearts, neither the farmer nor his wife could forget that Daphne was also the best guard dog they had ever kept!

On the night when the chicken thieves crept into the yard,

Daphne not only woke the farmer but pecked one of the thieves so badly on the nose that it has looked strangely like a beak ever since (and the police had very little difficulty in spotting the culprit later the same night).

When a boy drove one of the farmer's tractors right out of the yard just to prove that he could, Daphne sat herself firmly on his

head and wouldn't get off until
his mother arrived to take him
home and send him to bed
without any supper.

But it was with the apple-
stealers that Daphne really
excelled herself. She attacked
them so furiously that every
single one of the gang thought
that a whole flock of geese had
been let loose in the orchard. Of
course, it was night, so they
could not see that a solitary
duck on a mission dear to her
heart was pecking their knees
and flapping her wings in their
faces. Although the apple-
stealers were never caught, not

one of them ever troubled the
farmer again.

So that is why Daphne does
not now need to splash in the
animals' water troughs (though
she sometimes still does), or
steal the apples from the farmer's
kitchen (though she sometimes
still does), for she has her own
bowl of water in the orchard and
as many apples as she can eat
(which is a lot). Each spring, she
brings up a brood of ducklings
under the blossom-laden boughs.

And at three o'clock in the
morning? The farmer has bought
double-strength earplugs and
sleeps with a smile on his face.

The
Farmhouse
Mouse

When Farmer Brown had to fill in forms about who lived in the farmhouse at Daffodil Farm, this is what he put:

> David James Brown, 43 years
> Megan Sarah Brown, 40 years
> Matthew James Brown, 14 years
> Peter David Brown, 14 years
> Eleanor Jane Brown, 10 years
> Ben (sheepdog), 9 years
> Carla (cat), 7 years
> Barley (cat), 6 years
> Ruffles (guinea pig), 2 years
> Bubbles (goldfish), 1 year
> Mouse (mouse), who knows?

Perhaps you can tell from this list that of all the animals and people who lived with the farmer and his wife, only one gave him sleepless nights and anxious days. It was that wretched little mouse, who lived somewhere in the walls, or up in the attic, or under the floorboards, and who crept out almost every night and nibbled something or other in the farmhouse kitchen.

At night, the farmer lay awake and felt sure he could hear the pattering of tiny feet tiptapping down the stairs. Many times he had crept out of bed in his pyjamas and felt his way down into the kitchen without turning the light on, determined to catch that annoying little creature as it helped itself to yet another piece of pie or chunk of cheese.

But the farmer never so much as glimpsed a tiny twirly tail disappearing around a corner. Instead, he twice stubbed his toe on the hall table and once banged his nose *very* hard on a grandfather clock that he had forgotten was there.

There was no doubt about it. That mouse was just too clever for Farmer Brown, and although he tried to persuade all his family to help him catch the little scamperer, it was too clever for Mrs Brown, or the twins, or

Eleanor, or the dog, or the cats, or the hamster, or even the goldfish (although to be fair, as he could not leave his bowl, it would have been hard for him to help with this important project).

But, you will be asking, what *about* those cats? Isn't that one of the reasons that farmers keep cats – to catch mice? Well, when it came to catching mice, those cats were worse than useless. Carla was a great big fluffy white cat, so fat that she could hardly move. No self-respecting mouse would have been caught by Carla because you could hear her wheezing half a house away as she waddled towards you. Barley was not much better. He was a daredevil cat, and his exploits always ended in disaster. Barley was not content to sit quietly by a mouse-hole, waiting for its little occupant to emerge. Oh no. Barley had to climb up on to a cupboard on the opposite wall, ready to make a death-defying leap if he saw so much as a twitching whisker. Barley's leaps were famous in the farmhouse, because he hardly ever leapt alone. Sometimes it was saucepans, sometimes crockery, sometimes bags of flour that came crashing to the ground with him. By the time Barley had picked himself up and dusted himself down, any twitching whiskers had long since disappeared. The cats also put paid to the farmer's attempts to catch the mouse in a trap. First Carla, clumsily wandering into the kitchen, caught her fluffy tail in the trap and set up such a wailing that the whole house was woken. Then Barley, leaping from the table, jumped straight into the trap. He had sore toes for a month, which made his leaps even more destructive than before.

So the cats were no help at all, and the farmer regularly made threats to send them to the cats' home and buy a certified mouser who would rid him of the cheeky little pest once and for all.

Now I will tell you the real reason why the farmer never catches the farmhouse mouse, but you must promise never to tell him. *It's because there isn't one at all.* The pieces of pie, the chunks of cheese, the nibbles of this and that all go straight into the tummies of the dog, the cats, the hamster and even the goldfish. *They're* not going to tell the farmer that there are only ten inhabitants in the farmhouse. Are you?

Too Many Cats!

How many cats would you say were *too* many? Four? Six? Ten? Twenty-four? Mrs Martin, who lived at Maple Farm with her two daughters, *loved* cats. There were thirty-six of them on the farm, and she knew them all by name.

It had all started with two little kittens called Moppet and Poppet. After a couple of years, Moppet had four little kittens. After another couple of years, those kittens had kittens of their own, and so it went on. And as well as the cats that were born on Maple Farm, others came to visit and simply never seemed to go back to their own homes again. Mrs Martin counted them as permanent visitors.

One day the Government Vet came to call. He was happy with the contented pigs and the healthy cows. He approved of the way Mrs Martin was looking after her sheep and goats. He even gave a clean bill of health to the hens, ducks and geese. But when it came to cats, he drew the line.

"You have too many cats on the farm, Mrs Martin," he said. "Some of them will have to go."

"How many is too many?" asked Mrs Martin, just as I asked you at the beginning of the story.

"Shall we say that half of them must go?" suggested the vet. "I expect it to be done by the next time I call, in a month's time."

Mrs Martin went back into the farmhouse with her mouth set in a severe line. She poured herself a cup of tea and sat down in her chair with a *thump*.

"I'm not doing it," she said. "There is plenty of room on this farm for my cats – and more too if they arrive. They are all well fed and happy. Why should I get rid of any of them? And anyway, which ones would I choose? The old cats who have never known another home? Or the young ones who still need their mothers?"

Mrs Martin's daughters tried to persuade her to be sensible.

"That man can make you close down the farm, if you don't do as he says," they protested. "Can't you find good homes for some of the cats?"

"Good homes?" cried Mrs Martin. "Half of those cats came here because they were unhappy in their own homes. I can't send them out to people who may not take care of them. Do you think that's the kind of person I am? No, those cats are staying here."

Still, as the weeks passed, Mrs Martin did begin to feel a little

worried. Would the Government Vet really close down her farm? As the day of the next inspection drew near, all kinds of wild ideas passed through her mind. Could she hide half the cats until he was gone? Could she give him some of her cowslip wine, so that he wouldn't be able to count properly? Could she pretend to be ill and ask for more time? None of these ideas seemed very helpful.

The day of the Government Vet's visit dawned sunny and warm. Everywhere you looked around the farmyard there were cats lying in the sun or delicately licking their paws. It was the worst possible day for a cat count.

The Government Vet had a clipboard and a calculator. The Government Vet had sharp little eyes behind shiny spectacles. He spent two hours walking around the farm, making notes as he went.

When he arrived back at the farmhouse, Mrs Martin was waiting for him with a cup of tea.

"Thank you," said the G.V. "I needed that. Now, Mrs Martin, I have done a thorough count, and I find that you have exactly thirty-six cats. Does that agree with your figures?"

"Yes," said Mrs Martin faintly.

"Now," said the G.V., "I didn't do a full count before, so how many cats were there last time I called at Maple Farm?"

Mrs Martin crossed her fingers behind her back and suppressed a desire to giggle. It was going to be all right. She looked the Government Vet squarely in the eye and said without a blush, "Sir, there were seventy-two."

The Clever
Little
Rabbit

Nobody knew how the clever little rabbit came to be quite so clever. His parents were friendly, hardworking rabbits, but no one would have said they were particularly clever. In fact, the clever little rabbit's father got rather muddled if he had to count more than twenty-two cabbages at one time.

The clever little rabbit's brothers and sisters were quite ordinary little rabbits too. Tippytoes was well above average at hopping, but she could never remember if a hundred carrots was more than eight dozen. (It is.)

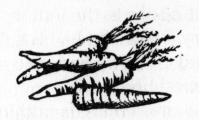

Twizzler had bigger ears than almost any rabbit you have ever seen, but he got stuck in the alphabet when he reached "f is for fox" (which is, after all, enough to frighten any young rabbit away from his letters.)

So the clever little rabbit's cleverness was a mystery. His name was Albert, but most rabbits called him Cleverclogs.

Before he had left the first class at school, Albert had read all the books in the junior library. Before he had left the second class, he had read all the teachers' books too.

"I'm afraid there is nothing more I can teach your son, Mr Nibbles," the headteacher told Albert's father. "He already knows more about maths and geography and carrot-crunching than I do."

Mr Nibbles was filled with pride, but he did rather wonder what to do with his extra-clever boy. After all, there is only so much maths and geography and carrot-crunching you can use in everyday life.

"Don't worry, Dad," said the clever little rabbit. "I'm setting up an Educational Emporium."

"A what?" asked his father. That sentence had contained at least two words that he didn't understand at all.

"An Educational Emporium," said Albert. "It's like a shop where you can find out all about everything."

"Shop" was a word that Mr Nibbles did understand. "You mean people give you money?" he asked.

"Yes," said Albert. "I hope so."

Mr Nibbles looked puzzled. "But what about stock, Albert?"

he asked. "You know, the stuff you're going to sell. How are you going to be able to buy that?"

"I know what stock is, Dad," laughed Albert. "And I don't have to buy it. It's all right up here." And he tapped his forehead in a mysterious manner.

Mr Nibbles still felt that he did not quite understand what Albert was proposing to do, but he soon found out the next day. In an empty tree-trunk house, Albert opened up his famous Educational Emporium.

His very first customer was his brother Twizzler. "Albert, I can't understand my maths homework

at all," he said. "Can your Ed …
Eju … can you help me?"

"Let me have a look," said the
clever little rabbit. "Yes, I see.
That will be two carrots, please,
Twizzler."

The price seemed cheap to
Twizzler, who had spent four
hours the night before puzzling
over his fractions. He willingly
handed over the carrots. In two
minutes flat, the clever little
rabbit had finished the problems
and even written them down in
something that looked very like
Twizzler's paw-writing.

Very soon, most of the
children at the school were

coming along to Albert to have their homework checked, finished, or just done from start to finish. Albert enjoyed the work and soon had more carrots, wizzo-balls and sweets than he really knew what to do with.

News of Albert's cleverness spread far and wide. Soon grown-up rabbits began to come to him as well. Old Farmer Fogarty brought over his accounts, which had caused him so much trouble that his whiskers were fraying. Albert took a day or two to sort them out, but Farmer Fogarty was really delighted with the result.

Aunt Jemima asked Albert to adjust her jam recipe, so that it made seventeen jars instead of eleven. The Bunny sisters regularly asked for help with the crossword in their newspaper. Miss Bunnyhop asked Albert to write all her letters to her boyfriend overseas, with the result that she became engaged within two weeks.

As the months and years passed, Albert became an essential part of life in the rabbit realm. There was even talk of calling the town Albertville. Albert was a very rich young rabbit, although to be fair, he hardly noticed how wealthy he had become. He was much more interested in solving problems and using his clever little brain.

One day, something happened to show that Albert's Educational Emporium was perhaps not quite such a good thing as everyone had thought. It was the middle of winter. Snow lay thick on the ground, and most sensible rabbits were snuggled deep in their burrows.

The wind blew and blew, whistling round the fields with an icy chill, blowing whirling snowflakes before it. When the storm finally stopped, the rabbits peeped out of their burrows to look at the strange, white world. It was then that they found that wind had pushed over a tree at the corner of a meadow, blocking the entrance to one large rabbit family's underground home.

Normally, the rabbits inside would have been able to dig themselves out, or the rabbits outside would have been able to dig themselves in, but the ground was so hard, it was quite impossible for any kind of digging to happen.

"We could write a note and push it down between the

branches, so that the rabbits inside know help is on its way," suggested Twizzler, as more and more rabbits gathered by the fallen tree.

"That's a good idea," said Mr Nibbles. "You write it, Twizzler."

But Twizzler looked rather embarrassed. The truth was that since Albert had set up his Educational Emporium, Twizzler hadn't written anything for himself at all. Now he had forgotten how! It soon became clear that none of the other rabbits could remember how to write proper letters either.

"I'll do it," said Albert quietly.

"Now," said Farmer Fogarty, taking charge of the practical side of things, "we're going to need some rope. Let's see. We'll need five metres here, and seven metres here, and fourteen metres for pulling. That makes ... er ... that's ... I never was much good at doing sums in my head."

The truth was that no one did sums at all any more, of course. Albert did them instead.

"We need twenty-six metres of rope," said Albert, thoughtfully.

It wasn't very long before the fallen tree had been pulled away and the trapped rabbits were rescued. The grateful family from the burrow below thanked all the rabbits for their help.

"We couldn't have done it without Albert," said Farmer Fogarty, and all the other rabbits agreed. But Albert seemed to have disappeared.

Next morning, Farmer Fogarty went along to the Educational Emporium to have his seed order written out as usual.

"I've brought a large bag of cabbages," he said. "I take it your charges haven't gone up recently, Albert?"

"No," said Albert, "but they have changed. Instead of a bag of cabbages, Farmer Fogarty, I will need you to do something for me in return for my help."

"What's that?" asked the old farmer in surprise.

"I will need you to help me with your seed order," said Albert. "I shall do some, and you will do some. We can finish it very quickly together."

Farmer Fogarty was doubtful, but by the time they had finished, he had remembered how to spell "seed" and "best" and "barley", so he felt pretty pleased with himself.

Over the weeks and months that followed, Albert helped his neighbours as usual, but he spent as much time showing them how to work out their own problems as he did solving them by himself.

Gradually, fewer and fewer rabbits made their way to Albert's door. The Educational Emporium was empty most of the day, but the rabbits who lived nearby were some of the cleverest rabbits you have ever met. Albert had less and less to do, although he still kept busy reading his books. Sometimes a whole week went by without a single rabbit knocking on the door. You might have thought that Albert would be worried,

but he looked as cheerful as ever.
Finally, the day came when Albert put a big sign on the door of the Educational Emporium.

CLOSED

Word flew round the town that Albert had gone out of business. Before the ink was dry on the notice, everyone had gathered outside the door of the famous Emporium to see what could be done to save it.

"We need you, Albert," said Twizzler.

"Why?" asked Albert.

"Well, to … and … or… well, I don't know."

It was true. The rabbits themselves could now do all the sums and letters and problems that Albert had helped with before. They really were very clever little rabbits.

"My job is over," said Albert. "The important thing about being clever is to pass on your cleverness to everyone else. It took me a long time to realise that, but I've been working hard, and I think I've done it now."

"But have you taught us everything you know?" asked Mr Nibbles, remembering an important conversation long ago with Albert's headteacher.

"Well, no," said Albert. "But what else is there that you would *like* to know?"

"I was thinking of Evening Classes," said Mr Nibbles firmly. "I've always had a great wish to learn Chinese. There are a lot of rabbits in China, you know."

"I was thinking of Advanced Carrot Arranging," said Miss Honeybun.

"I would be interested in a course on meaty ... meaty-o ...

meaty-o-algy," said young Twizzler, hesitantly.

"Meaty-o-algy?"

"You know, about the weather," explained Twizzler.

Albert smiled. "Courses in Chinese, Carrot Arranging and Meteorology will begin next week," he said. "Now, if you will excuse me, I have some studying to do."

You will be glad to know that the Educational Emporium is flourishing, and Albert has never been happier. It takes a very clever little rabbit to solve everyone else's problems, but it takes an even cleverer rabbit to show others how to solve their own problems. And Albert, as you know, was a very clever little rabbit indeed.

The
Unhappy
Elephant

Once upon a time, there was an unhappy elephant. He was so unhappy that all the other animals in the jungle were miserable too.

Early in the morning, the monkeys would be disturbed in their treetops by a big, sad, booming sound.

"Boo hoo! Boo hoo!"

The noise shook the leaves and the mangoes from the trees.

"There goes our breakfast again!" sighed one monkey. "Something has got to be done about that elephant."

In another part of the jungle, high in the branches of a

glubglub tree, the parrots were squawking together.

"What are we going to do about that elephant?" they asked each other. "He's got to cheer up. We can't go on like this."

"Very true, very true," whistled the little singing birds in the branches above.

"Ssssoooo," hissed the tree snake, slithering around a nearby trunk. "What's the trouble with the ssssssobbing one?"

For a whole minute, the chattering birds were silent. They were never quite sure if they could trust the slithering snake, who moved so silently.

At last an older parrot shuffled his feet on his perch.

"Well, we don't really know," he said. "It all started a few weeks ago. He was a perfectly happy elephant before that."

"Then I ssssuggest that ssssomeone finds out," said the snake, sliding silently away to find his breakfast.

The birds looked at each other. Then they all spoke at once.

"This is a job for a monkey," they said.

When the wisest monkey of all was told what they wanted, he agreed at once with their unanimous decision.

"You're quite right," he said. "Someone must talk to the poor animal and find out what is wrong. Then, perhaps, we can do something to put it right. But let me have my breakfast first. For this kind of job, I will need to be on top form."

So the monkey munched some mangoes. Then he didn't feel quite ready to face the elephant, so he snacked on a couple of bananas. Still, the idea of talking to a sad elephant wasn't very appealing, so he swung over to another part of the jungle and found some of his favourite green leaves. By the time he had finished those, he was almost too full to do anything.

"I think I'll just have a little sleep," he said, "so that I'll be fresh and my wits will be sharp for talking to that elephant."

The other monkeys sat in their treetops and listened. The sounds of the sad elephant still echoed through the jungle.

"Boo hoo! Boo hoo!"

"It doesn't sound as if anyone is talking to him," said the youngest monkey in a puzzled little voice.

"Excuse me," said the wisest monkey's wife. "I think I know what may have happened." She hurried off across the jungle and found her husband sleeping peacefully in the branches of a glubglub tree. He was not sleeping peacefully for long...

So it was that the wisest monkey had a rather pink face as he swung down into the clearing where the elephant was still sadly sniffling.

"Boo hoo! Boo hoo!" said, the elephant, more quietly now.

The wisest monkey cleared his throat and tried to look kindly and, if not wise, at least reasonably clever. He was very aware that the elephant was several hundred times larger than he was. There were stories in the past of elephants carelessly plonking one of their great feet on a monkey's tail, with tragic results. With this in mind, the wisest monkey stayed well out of the way on a branch level with the elephant's eyes.

"Ahem! I couldn't help noticing, old chap…" began the monkey, scratching himself in a way that was meant to look as if he was relaxed and confident. In fact, to an elephant, it made him look particularly nervous and shifty. The elephant moved his great weight from foot to foot and waited for the monkey to continue. He did not think it was likely that the monkey could have anything interesting to say.

"Well, it isn't just me," said the monkey. "Several of your jungle friends have noticed that you're not … well, that is, you're very … I mean to say, you're a bit…"

"You mean I'm miserable," said the elephant, in a low, rumbling voice that quivered in a rather desperate kind of way.

"Miserable? Yes. Good word. Miserable. That's a fine way of putting it," said the monkey, encouragingly.

"It's not a very fine way of feeling," said the elephant.

"No, no, of course not. Not a fine way of feeling at all. But might I ask … that is, if I could be so bold as to enquire … in fact, I wonder if you would be good enough to tell me…"

"Why I'm so miserable?" asked the large grey animal.

"Yes, yes. That's it exactly." The monkey tried to take a grip and put on his most professional tones. "Now what exactly seems to be the trouble?" he asked.

"I'm too fat," said the elephant.

"What?" The monkey couldn't believe his ears. "Feeling flat, did you say?" he queried. "Everyone does at some time, you know."

"No. I'm too *fat*. Too round. Too heavy. Too solid. Too much of me. Too fat."

"Oh," said the monkey, "that kind of too fat. I see."

But in truth he did not see. Too fat? An elephant? It wasn't possible. Whoever heard of a thin elephant?

"What makes you think so?" he asked at last, a hundred questions still buzzing in his brain.

"It's obvious," replied the elephant. "Name me one animal in the whole wide world who's bigger than me! Have you ever seen one? No, I thought not. How would you like to be the fattest animal on earth? Would that make you happy?"

The wisest monkey really could not think of anything to say to that. The idea of being the fattest monkey on earth was not very appealing. The idea of being an elephant was not appealing either (for they are notoriously bad at climbing trees). On the other hand, the idea of being a fat elephant did not sound so very awful. If you had to be an elephant, surely it was better to be a fat elephant?

As he could think of no reassuring words, the monkey risked a quick pat on the huge elephant's trunk and swung off through the branches to report back to the other animals.

"Well?" asked the parrot. "What's the matter with the old fellow?"

The wisest monkey explained. Then he explained again.

Then, as no one seemed able to believe what he said, he led the parrot and the other monkeys and the little singing birds and the tree snake to the elephant's clearing and let them hear for themselves.

What a twittering and a chattering and a hissing there was! Everyone tried to talk at once, but no one could think of a single sensible thing to say to the elephant.

Except one. The old parrot fluttered on his jewelled wings to a nearby branch and spoke with authority.

"My dear friend," he said, "where would we all be without your majestic size? Who was it who pushed over that tree last year when our smallest monkey got trapped inside the trunk? Who gave a mighty shake to the nuggle-nut tree, so that its nuts came tumbling down from the highest branches? Who frightened away that lean, low leopard when he came visiting only a month ago, looking at little birds and monkeys with his glittering eyes? Who stamped out the first sparks of a dreadful forest fire with his beautiful big feet? It was you, my friend. None of the rest of us could have done any of those things."

"So you think it's all right to be the largest animal on earth?" quavered the elephant, shuffling.

"I'm sorry to tell you," replied the parrot, nodding his rainbow head wisely, "that you are not the largest animal on earth by any means. That great honour – and it is an honour indeed – goes to the blue whale, an animal so huge that it cannot live on land at all. It does not have legs, for no legs could support its mighty size. It swims in the oceans."

"Then how does anyone know it is there?" asked the elephant, curious in spite of himself.

"From time to time," replied the parrot, "the whale rises to the surface of the sea to breathe, for it is not a fish but an animal like ourselves. When it breathes out, a great spurt of water flies up from the top of its head, higher in the air than our highest jungle trees. It comes out with a kind of a woosh!"

"Like the spurting I can do from my trunk?" asked the elephant with interest.

"Very like," said the parrot.

"Then I have a big cousin in the sea," smiled the elephant. "I don't know why you call him a whale, for he is clearly an ocean elephant, the greatest of us all."

"Ha, ha!" agreed the parrot. "You see, my friend, that bigness is nothing to be afraid of at all."

"I see that clearly now," agreed the elephant. "I see, indeed, that I am not too big but too small. If you will excuse me, I must have my breakfast at once. There is some serious eating to be done."

And he wandered happily off in search of fruit and leaves.

"There'll be nothing left for the rest of us," groaned the other animals as soon as he was gone.

"He may even find my secret mango store," agreed the wisest monkey. "Why did you have to open your big beak, parrot? This was quite obviously a job for monkeys!"

"He will be sssstamping his great feet everywhere," hissed the tree snake.

If there is a moral to this story, it is that you can't keep everybody happy all the time. That a monkey is still a monkey, however wise he is. And that we should all feel very happy indeed that blue whales do not have legs. Or there would be no mangoes left for the rest of us – none at all!

The
Sheep
Shambles

You probably know the nursery rhyme about Little Bo Peep. That silly girl lost all her sheep and didn't know where to find them. In the end, they came home again, but not before she had had some very worrying moments and one or two sleepless nights.

Once there was a shepherd who was very, very anxious about losing his sheep. Of course, every shepherd is concerned about this, but young Douglas McDougal had rather a reputation for losing parts of his flock. It wasn't really his fault. Some sheep are just plain contrary, and if they could fall into gullies or get stuck behind boulders, you can be sure that Douglas McDougal's sheep would. He was supposed to have a hundred sheep, but very often one or two of them wandered off for a while.

Luckily, because he was a hardworking shepherd, he usually found them again, but that didn't stop his friends from laughing at him. They called him "Little Bo Peep" and chuckled whenever they saw him. Douglas McDougal was determined he would never have another mishap in all his days on the hillside.

In the summertime, it was not so very difficult. Douglas McDougal and his dog, called Jem, could look out across the green hillside and know that every white dot was a sheep or a lamb. It was quite easy to count them and make sure that there were none missing, especially in the middle of the day, when it was hot. Many sheep are not very energetic animals at the best of times, and in hot weather they are not so keen to run races or jump over streams.

"Ninety-seven, ninety-eight … don't interrupt me, Jem … ninety-nine, one hundred! They're all there!" Douglas McDougal would say with a smile, as he sat with his sandwiches under the only tree on the hill.

Then Jem would allow himself ten minutes' snooze in the sunshine, before he ran off to check that none of the stragglers had strayed.

In this way, Douglas McDougal and Jem managed not to lose a

single sheep all summer. In fact, they actually found one that had strayed from another flock, although they returned it at once.

Still Douglas McDougal's friends made fun of him.

"How many sheep have you lost today, Bo Peep?" they would call. "Where's your bonnet?"

Douglas McDougal began to dread the winter, for then the whole hillside was covered with snow. It can be very hard to see a white sheep among the white snow. What was he going to do?

Douglas McDougal thought long and hard. He considered radio transmitters around the sheep's necks. He thought about painting numbers on their backs and hiring a helicopter. He wondered if he could train them to make a specially loud bleating sound so that he could track them down. He considered putting them in fluorescent cycling jackets. He even thought about tying leads to their legs, so that he could pull the bleating strays through the snow towards him.

None of these ideas was really possible. Most of them, to be sure, were rather silly. In the end, Douglas McDougal decided to ask his friend Hamish Hamish for advice.

Now Hamish Hamish was an inventor who lived in Douglas McDougal's village. He had a reputation for being a very clever man. Like many inventors, Hamish Hamish was brimming with ideas. Half of them were brilliant. Half of them were crazy. The really difficult thing was telling which were which. His porridge-pourer, for example, had worked really well, and was used by several of the hotels round about. His haggis-heater, on the other hand, had caused several serious explosions and considerable damage to the roof of the village store.

Still, Douglas McDougal was desperate, so he explained his problem to Hamish Hamish. It didn't take the inventor long to come up with an idea.

"The problem is," he said, "that sheep are white and snow is white."

"I know that," said Douglas McDougal.

"One of them," cried Hamish Hamish, "will have to change."

"You think I should spray the snow a different colour?" asked Douglas McDougal.

"No," replied the inventor. "I think you should change the colour of your sheep."

"Now look," said Douglas McDougal rather heatedly. "One of the reasons I am anxious not to lose any sheep is so that my friends don't laugh at me. What do you think they will say if I suddenly turn up with pink or green sheep? I'd never hear the end of it."

"I was thinking of a lovely shade of turquoise," said Hamish Hamish coldly. "And you wouldn't need to worry about your friends. During the coldest weather, they will be more than busy looking after their own sheep on their own hillsides. No one but you will see your sheep until spring, and by then the colour will have faded away completely."

This sounded quite sensible. "You're quite sure that the colour will disappear?" asked Douglas McDougal.

"It is not affected by wet," said Hamish Hamish, "but it fades to white in warm sunshine. In spring you will have the whitest, brightest sheep anyone in the hills has ever seen."

So Douglas McDougal went home with a packet of powder, which he put in the sheep's water as Hamish Hamish had instructed.

"It won't work at once," said the inventor. "But as soon as the weather becomes really cold, you will see the difference."

Douglas McDougal watched his sheep carefully. They looked just the same as ever. Then, one night, there was a sharp frost. In the morning, when the shepherd went to look at his flock, he saw a hillside covered with little blancmanges. There was no doubt about it. The sheep were pink!

Douglas McDougal left Jem in charge and stormed off to Hamish Hamish's house at once.

"The sheep are not," he said, "a lovely shade of turquoise.

They are pink, and it is not a subtle shade."

"Salmon?" asked Hamish Hamish. "Rose-petal? Blush? Peach?"

"The term I would use," said the shepherd, "is puce."

"Hmmm," said Hamish Hamish, "not quite turquoise then, but still very visible against the snow, and that, after all, is the point of the exercise. Let's not get carried away with irrelevancies, young Douglas."

Young Douglas went back to his sheep, and even he had to admit that he had no trouble keeping track of them that winter. He was interested to see that the new lambs that were born were just as bright a colour as their mothers, so he had no trouble looking after them either.

As winter passed, and the first sunshine of spring began to filter palely through the clouds, Douglas McDougal waited with some anxiety to see what would happen to the colour of his well-tended sheep.

"The change will come any day now," Hamish Hamish assured him. "Have patience, my boy."

One morning, the inventor found Douglas McDougal waiting for him when he drew back his bedroom curtains.

"The change has come," said the shepherd grimly. "I'd like you to come and see."

Without giving the inventor time to change out of his dressing gown, Douglas dragged Hamish Hamish down the road and up into the hills. There, spread across the hillside, were Douglas McDougal's sheep. A finer flock you never did see, and they were not pink. No, they were blue and purple and red and orange and yellow and green. In fact, they were every single colour of the rainbow.

"Ah," said the inventor. "Ah, now, yes, I see."

"What exactly do you see?" asked the shepherd, icily.

"I see two that are absolutely the lovely shade of turquoise I was thinking of," said Hamish Hamish in a squeaky voice.

"What exactly," asked Douglas McDougal, in a voice that was, if anything, even colder, "do you suggest that I do?"

"A hot wash and an extra-long rinse cycle?" queried Hamish Hamish. "Bleach? Little white jackets to cover them from foot to tail? A big shock to turn their hair white? Emigration?"

He was already halfway down the road, as Douglas McDougal raised his shepherd's crook in what can only be described as a threatening manner.

Douglas McDougal knew that it was only a matter of time before his friends climbed up to his hillside and discovered the awful truth about his flock.

But next day, as the young shepherd climbed wearily up to his flock, he was astonished to see that his secret had already been discovered. There seemed to be more people on the hillside than sheep! Several television cameras and a whole crowd of news photographers were crowding round an orange lamb, while men with clipboards tried unsuccessfully to herd sheep of different attractive colours to stand next to each other.

"I need another yellow one!" a man in a tweed jacket was calling. "No, no, the magenta will clash. Oh, all right, blue will do."

As Douglas McDougal approached, a woman in a long scarf ran up to him with a microphone.

"Mr McDougal," she cried, "how does it feel to be named the Young Entrepreneur of the Year for your Ready-Dyed Wool Production?"

"My what?" asked Douglas.

"Your coloured sheep," explained the woman in the scarf. "Have you not heard about your prize?"

It soon became clear that, far from laughing at Douglas McDougal, everyone wanted sheep just like his. Overnight, he was famous, and his sheep were in great demand.

"How did you do it, Douglas?" the news reporters asked him.

"I don't know…" began the shepherd, but Hamish Hamish could be heard behind him.

"It was the result of years of work," he said. "I'm Hamish Hamish, Mr McDougal's Research and Development Officer. How big did you say the prize was?"

Well, Douglas McDougal is a rich man now and is quite happy to be called Little Bo Peep if that is what people want to do, but he still gets a little nervous when the sun shines.

The Bothering Buzz

There was once an old man who lived by himself in the country. He had no neighbours for miles around.

"Don't you feel lonely?" asked his sister, when she visited from the town at the end of the valley.

"Not at all," replied Mr Billings. "What I need more than anything else is peace and quiet to do my work. I couldn't have that with neighbours popping in and out all the time, could I?"

"But what if you get ill," his sister went on. "We might not know for weeks and weeks. You could be lying on the floor, moaning and groaning."

"You know perfectly well," her brother replied, "that I'm as strong as an ox. Nothing is going to happen to me, but to put your mind at rest, why don't we have a signal?"

"A signal?" said his sister. "What kind of signal?"

"Your little boy has a brand new telescope, doesn't he?"

"Yes, but what…?"

"Look through the telescope at ten o'clock every morning, and, if I'm not well, I'll light a fire and make a smoke signal. If you see smoke rising from the cottage, you'll know I'm not well – or the cottage is on fire, of course. In either case, your assistance will be very gratefully received."

Mr Billings' sister had to be satisfied with that, but she still went home shaking her head over her brother's stubbornness.

Mr Billings went happily back into his cottage and sat down with his books. He was writing an encyclopedia of natural history, which he knew would take him years to complete. That didn't worry Mr Billings. He enjoyed his work so much that he looked forward to sitting down with his books each morning. Not many people are lucky enough to be so happy in their work as Mr Billings, even if he *was* still on "a" for "ant".

Mr Billings' days passed peacefully in his country cottage. He would get up at dawn, when the sun was just peeping over the horizon, and make himself some tea. Then he would go straight to his desk and delve once more into the fascinating world of plants, animals and insects. In fact, he very often forgot to eat his lunch *or* his supper, but he munched happily at the apples that grew on the tree outside his window, and his sister would send him a large fruit cake at least once a week.

Meanwhile, Mr Billings sister was following the plan that he had outlined. Every morning at ten o'clock, she borrowed her son's telescope and peered out of the window with it. She became so skilled that she could pick her brother's cottage out from among the trees in five seconds flat. There never was any smoke curling from the chimney, so she felt happy that Mr Billings was safe and well.

For six months, Mr Billings worked quietly away. He had reached "b" for "barnacles" and was particularly fascinated by the way that barnacles cling on to the bottoms of ships, hitching rides around the world.

One morning, Mr Billings was drawing a map to show the journey of one particularly adventurous barnacle, when his concentration was disturbed by a buzzing sound.

"Buzz! Buzz!" it went, right next to his ear. Mr Billings flapped his hands wildly around his head. It sounded as though there was an insect hovering just behind him.

The buzzing stopped, and Mr Billings continued with his work. But just as he was turning the page of one of his books, he heard the annoying sound again.

"Buzz! Buzz!"

Mr Billings stood up. If there was one thing he needed, it was peace and quiet, and this buzzing was driving him mad. He looked around very, very carefully, using his magnifying glass to search in the corners, and at last he found the cause of the bothering buzz.

A little brown bee was sitting on the edge of his desk.

"Buzz!" it said, in a friendly way. "Buzz!"

"This won't do, you know," said Mr Billings. "This won't do at all. I cannot have my work interrupted by this buzz, buzz, buzzing. Can't you be quieter, little bee?"

The bee did its very, very best. "Buzz!" it said. "Buzz! Buzz!"

But Mr Billings had very sensitive ears. Even when the bee was buzzing as quietly as it knew how, he could still hear it.

"I'm afraid you're going to have to go outside, my friend," said

Mr Billings. "And please try not to come inside my cottage again, because I really don't want to hurt you. You are such a little bee, and I am such a big Billings that it might be a disaster if I sat on you by mistake."

The little bee privately thought that the disaster might not be all on one side. After all, Mr Billings might not feel so cheerful with a sting on his big bottom!

Mr Billings opened the window, and out flew the bee. The kindly old gentleman went back to his work and was soon lost in his undersea world again, where there are no bees at all.

Half an hour later, Mr Billings' work was rudely interrupted.

"Buzz! BUZZ!" came a noise in his ear, much, much louder than last time.

"It's that blessed bee again!" cried Mr Billings, picking up his magnifying glass. This time he found the little creature much more quickly. It was perched right on the end of his pencil!

"Now, you know," said Mr Billings rather angrily, "that you and I discussed this matter only a few minutes ago. And I thought that we had an understanding. Bees outside. Billings inside. That was how it went."

But as Mr Billings looked closely at the bee, he began to feel sure that this was not the same bee that he had talked with before. This bee was a little darker in colour and rather smaller than the first one.

"I'm sorry," said Mr Billings, who did like to be fair when he could, "perhaps we haven't met. But I'm afraid I shall have to tell you what I told your friend. I really cannot have buzzing in my ears when I am working. It is most distressing. Now buzz off like a good little bee and let me get on. And you might like to tell your friends what I have told you."

I'm sure you don't need me to tell you what happened for the rest of the afternoon. Over and over again, Mr Billings was disturbed by a buzz, buzz, buzzing. When he looked at his visitor with his magnifying glass, he was almost sure each time that it was a different bee from the time before.

Of course, it is not easy to recognise different bees, unless you are a bee yourself, so Mr Billings became rather confused before the end of the afternoon. Finally, at his wits' end, he decided to look up the subject of bees in one of his books.

What he read there was not very encouraging. He discovered something that he would have known already if he had paused to think for two minutes earlier that day. Bees do not live alone, as Mr Billings did. They live in swarms of hundreds or maybe thousands of bees, all of them busily bustling and buzzing about all day long.

Mr Billings put down his book. So there was a swarm of bees somewhere very near his cottage. So the bee visitors were very likely to continue. So the buzzing was very *un*likely to stop. Whatever could he do? Mr

Billings went to bed that night with a heavy heart.

"I've been very happy in this little cottage," he said to himself. "I really don't want to have to move away, but what is the alternative? I can't possibly work here with all this buzzing. Wait a minute, perhaps that's the answer! If I am not to move, then the bees must move instead!"

Mr Billings was so excited about his idea that he could not stay in bed. He bounced up and sat late into the night, reading his books about insects.

In the morning, he didn't even wait for his breakfast tea, but set

out straight away for the town,
to make some special purchases.

Mr Billings returned home that
afternoon with a large cardboard
box and a small pumping
machine. It was too late to begin
work that day, but he went to
bed confident that his troubles
would soon be at an end.

Next morning, Mr Billings
searched in his old chests and
found his ancient insect-hunting
outfit from his days on the
Amazon. He put on some gloves,
a long-sleeved shirt, long
trousers and some boots. Then
he put a large hat on his head. It
had a net hanging all the way

round it, so that insects couldn't creep under it and sting him on the nose!

Ready at last, Mr Billings picked up his cardboard box and his pumping machine and went outside. It did not take very long to find the swarm of bees. Mr Billings simply followed the sound of buzzing until he came to one of his old apple trees. There, high in the branches, Mr Billings could see a huge mass of bees clinging together.

Mr Billings made his last-minute preparations. With the box under one arm and the pumping machine held firmly in

his hand, he began slowly to climb the ladder leaning against the tree. Inch by inch, he climbed, as quietly as a cat.

One or two bees buzzed around to look at this strange creature who was approaching their home, but he looked harmless enough.

As soon as he was near enough to the mass of bees, Mr Billings opened his cardboard box and lodged it safely on a broad branch. Then he pointed his pumping machine at the bees and pumped for all he was worth.

It was a smoke machine. Mr Billings' books had told him that the smoke would make the bees drowsy, so that he could catch them in the box and take them to someone who could look after them in a proper hive. It worked like a charm. The sleepy bees dropped into the box, and even the stray ones followed them, so they were not left behind.

As quickly as he could with his gloved hands, Mr Billings fastened the cardboard box and carried it carefully down the tree. He put it on the back seat of his car while he went inside to change out of his insect-catching clothes and hat.

As he changed, Mr Billings took a deep breath and listened hard. Nothing! Not a buzz could be heard anywhere in the still and silent cottage.

"Peace at last!" said Mr Billings.
Drrrriiiiiiinnnng! Drrrriiiiiinnnng!
Beeeeeebaaaa! Beeeeeebaaaa!"

An atrocious nose assaulted Mr Billings' ears. It was hundreds of times worse than any buzzing he had ever heard.

Mr Billings was so confused for a moment, he almost didn't notice the hammering on his front door.

When he opened it, he was amazed to see two burly firemen, a policeman and two ambulance drivers standing outside.

"Step aside, Sir," said one of the firemen. "We'll soon have this under control. Which way?"

"Which way to what?" asked Mr Billings.

"To the fire!" said the fireman. "Don't waste our time, please."

"What fire?" cried Mr Billings. "There isn't any fire."

"That's not what this lady says," said the fireman sternly. He moved back to reveal ... Mr Billings' sister!

"Oh George," she sobbed. "I thought something dreadful had happened to you."

Yes, that morning, Mr Billings' sister had picked up her son's telescope as usual and looked out towards her brother's cottage. You can imagine her concern when she saw lots and lots of white smoke billowing from the cottage. At least, it looked as if it were coming from the cottage, for, of course, it never entered her head that so much smoke could be coming from an apple tree!

Mr Billings' sister lost no time. She rang up all the emergency services and set off herself at once. She was determined to save her brother at all costs. As she drove along, she couldn't help remembering her brother's little joke. "If you see smoke rising from the cottage, you'll know I'm not well – or the cottage is on fire, of course." How little she had dreamed that his laughing words would come true! Thank goodness she had agreed to that silly signal!

Now Mr Billings' quiet cottage was surrounded by vehicles and people. *Woooooosh!* a stream of water flooded through his open bedroom window (and straight on to his bed below), as one of the younger firemen got rather enthusiastic with the hose.

It took some time for all the explanations to be made, but everything worked out quite well in the end. One of the ambulance drivers turned out to be an

expert on bees and happily took them away to put in his own hive.

Even the firemen and the policeman were not too cross.

"It's good to do an exercise like this from time to time," said the policeman. "But don't make a habit of it."

When everyone had gone, Mr Billings' sister turned to her brother and apologised.

"It's not your fault, my dear," he said. "I'll go and make us both a nice cup of tea. You'll feel better after that."

Later, as they sat under the apple tree and Mr Billings' sister's knees had almost stopped shaking, he begged her again not to worry.

"You were only trying to look after me," he said. "I'm a very lucky man to have someone like you. But we are going to need a much better signalling system in the future, aren't we?"

"What did you have in mind?" asked his sister anxiously. "It will take me a little while to learn semaphore or morse code. Or were you thinking of something more complicated?"

"Not at all, my dear," laughed Mr Billings. "I was thinking of doing something I should have done months ago. I was thinking of buying a telephone!"

The Inquisitive Parrot

Once upon a time, there was a parrot who simply could not mind his own business. If he heard two monkeys discussing their sister's cousin's new baby, he would have to poke his rather large beak right into the private conversation.

"What did they call the baby?" he would squawk. "Evangeline is a nice name, especially for a monkey. Or what about Annabel or Gwendoline?"

The monkeys would shuffle along their branch a little to try to escape from the annoying eavesdropper, but the parrot never noticed hints of that kind.

"Christabel is also a lovely name. My aunt's brother-in-law called his second daughter that. I thought it was terribly pretty. What do you think?"

The monkeys would look at each other in despair. The only way to get rid of the parrot was to be downright rude to him, but no one wants to do that if it can be helped.

"I'm also very fond of Carmelita. So charming. And Madeleine has a very sweet sound, too."

Finally, of course, one of the monkeys would simply have to look the inquisitive parrot in the eye and tell him to mind his own business. "We were having a private conversation," she would say, "and now you have spoilt it, so we are leaving. And just in *case* you're interested, and I'm sure you *will* be, the baby was a boy, and they're calling him Karl."

Do you think the parrot was upset at being spoken to in this way? Did he ruffle his feathers and sidle away, hanging his brilliant green head? Not a bit of it. The whole thing was like water off a … well, off a *parrot's* back. As the monkeys moved off, you might hear him muttering to himself. "Hmmm, Karl. That's not a bad name at all. In fact, I'm sure I remember my mother telling me, oh, it must be years ago now, that her cousin…"

That was how it went on, day after day, deep in the jungle. Now the jungle, as you probably know, is usually a very sociable place. Everyone knows everyone else, and there is more gossip and chattering to be heard among the huge green leaves than almost anywhere else on earth. Of course, some of the larger animals are not such great chatterers – you won't often find a leopard discussing the weather with an elephant, for example –

but most of the time, the animals all get along together pretty well.

Perhaps that is why the other animals put up with the parrot as well as they did. He was an incredibly nosey bird, but he didn't really mean any harm by it. It was simply that if there was something going on, then he had to know about it. And he wouldn't rest until he had found out, even if everyone was quite determined to keep the secret.

The trouble with secrets, as I'm sure you know, is that they are really no good at all unless you can *tell* someone about them. I mean, what is the use of knowing a particularly good secret if you can't let someone else know that you know it? And then, of course, once they know that you know something, they will not rest until you have told *them* too.

"Well, I will tell *you*," we say, "but you must promise me not to tell anyone else at all."

It never quite works, does it? That someone has to tell just one other someone, and so on, and so on.

That was why the parrot really didn't have too much trouble finding out about everything that was going on, whether the others wanted him to know or not.

One day, one of the little singing birds who lived at the top of the nuggle-nut tree discovered a very important secret indeed. The elephant whose big grey shape could often be seen wandering across the jungle clearings was about to have a birthday, and it was rather an important birthday, too. He was going to be seventy years old, which is a very great age for an elephant, and certainly something that should be celebrated.

"We should have a party," said the little singing birds. "And all the animals will be invited. We'll

pick some beautiful flowers to make into a garland for the elephant. He will look so very handsome with it round his neck."

"We can collect lots of lovely green leaves for everyone to eat," said the monkeys, "and some nuts and fruit as well, of course."

"What about a birthday song?" asked the singing birds, who, as you can see, were really entering into the spirit of the occasion. "We could sing a special Happy Birthday song for him."

"We're not very good at singing," said the monkeys, "but we could put on an acrobatic display, swooping through the branches while you sang your song, perhaps. What do you think? Would he like that?"

It was generally agreed that the elephant would like that very much indeed.

Then one of the monkeys said what several of the animals had been thinking.

"Er ... it *is* supposed to be a surprise, isn't it?" she asked.

"Yes," agreed the singing birds, all twittering together. "The elephant mustn't know anything about it until the great day."

"So that means," said the monkey, "that we must be very, very careful not to let him know, even by the slightest little hint. We will need to very careful."

Everyone could see where the conversation was leading. One little monkey was brave enough to say it.

"So we are agreed, then, that the parrot must not be told about this. Am I right?"

There was no shortage of voices to agree with *that*. Of course, agreeing *not* to do something is much, much easier than putting the agreement into practice. Over and over again, during the weeks that followed, the parrot would just happen to be around when something important was being discussed. It was quite obvious to him that a Really Big Secret was lurking somewhere in the jungle, and he felt quite sure it was his duty to find it.

The parrot found his first clue late one night, when the stars were twinkling in the dark sky above the trees. At night the jungle is full of sounds.

As the parrot looked up at the night sky, he heard a little chirping sound far above him. As quietly as he could, he hopped up through the branches until he was nearer to the sound. It was very, very soft, but he thought he heard, floating through the dark leaves, just a few words.

"Happy Birthday, dear hmmm hmm hmm,
Happy Birthday to youuuoooo!"

The parrot shook his head. It wasn't anybody's birthday today, surely? And anyway, why would those little singing birds be celebrating a birthday in the middle of the night? They were usually fast asleep by this time.

Unless … unless they were practising! That must be it. They were practising a birthday song for someone very special.

The parrot pecked thoughtfully at his feathers. He couldn't think of anyone who had a birthday about now. In fact, like most animals, he couldn't even remember when his own birthday was. It is usually only animals who are very good at remembering things – such as elephants – who celebrate their birthdays at all.

The parrot wished he could creep closer to the little singing birds, but he was afraid of being heard. He was a rather large parrot and not very good at creeping silently through the leaves. Besides, the branches at the top of the trees were very, very, thin. He thought they might well not bear the weight of a rather plump parrot.

Next morning, as he was going about his business as usual (which really means, as he was going about putting his beak into everyone else's business), the parrot was nearly knocked off his perch by a monkey swinging by.

Woooosh! Just as he regained his balance, another one hurtled past, and *Woooooosh! Wooooosh!*

Wooooooosh! another and another and another.

The parrot scuttled down to a fallen log near the ground, where he felt safer. What on earth was going on? Those monkeys were well known to be rather lazy in the mornings. Here they were swooping and wooping through thebranches as though they were showing off to someone very important.

Just then, the parrot heard one of the monkeys call to another, high up above his head.

"If you start your swing a little earlier, I can catch you just as you pass over you-know-who's head. It will look much more impressive. Trust me!"

"All right," called another monkey. "But if you drop me, you can peel your own bananas from now on!"

The parrot hopped up and down with excitement. Those monkeys were putting on a show! They were going to do a special performance for someone very important. Whoever could it be?

The parrot thought and thought. Perhaps a famous animal of some kind was going to visit the jungle. But in that case, why didn't he know about it? The more the parrot thought, the more he felt sure that the other animals were deliberately keeping secrets not just from anyone, but from *him*! It seemed very strange.

That night, the parrot could not sleep. In his mind, he kept going over and over the clues he had picked up. From something a baby monkey had let slip, he felt sure that the great event was to happen the following afternoon. What could it be?

It was then that the parrot suddenly hit upon a solution that would explain why he was the last to know about the surprise birthday treat. It must be his *own* birthday! That was the only possible reason for all this secrecy. The animals were going to surprise him!

Now, if he had stopped to think about it a little more, the parrot might have realised that if he didn't know himself when his birthday was, the chances were that the other animals wouldn't know either. But he didn't stop to think. He was so filled up with pride and excitement that not another sensible thought went through his feathery head the whole night.

Next morning, the parrot was beside himself with excitement.

There was hustling and bustling everywhere, as all the animals prepared their various suprises. The parrot peered round leaves and peeped under branches, but he only saw the most tantalising glimpses of what was being done. He wondered where he should spend the rest of the morning. He didn't, after all, want to make it difficult for the other animals to *find* him when the time came. With that in mind, the parrot went to sit right in the middle of the biggest clearing in the jungle, which was, in fact, the very one that the animals had chosen for the elephant's party.

"What's he doing sssssitting *there*?" hissed the tree snake. "He's in the way as ussssssual. What are we going to do?"

"Someone will have to have a word with him," said one of the monkeys. "It's probably time he was told, anyway. He can't really do anything to spoil it all now. My cousin is making sure the elephant has a long, muddy bath this morning, so that he doesn't come back and find out what's going on."

The monkey swung down into the clearing and ambled over to the parrot, who was trying to look casual, as though he sat around in the middle of an open space every day of the week.

"Hello, there," said the monkey. "A word in your ear, old friend. There's something we think you should know."

"No, no," said the parrot, blushing and holding up a wing. "You don't have to say anything. I've guessed your secret already, and I must say, I think it's a wonderful idea. I'm very touched. Very touched, indeed."

"Are you?" asked the monkey, surprised. He hadn't realised that the parrot was quite so fond of the elephant. After all, there had been that time when he got squirted by mistake and had to spend a whole week drying out his feathers.

"So ... er ... were you thinking of waiting here until..." began the monkey. "Because there are one or two things we need to get ready, you know."

"Oh," squawked the parrot. "Yes, of course. I'm sorry. I'm in the way. I'll come back, shall I, this afternoon?"

"That would be perfect," said the monkey. "Don't be late!"

"Oh, I wouldn't dream of it," chuckled the parrot. Late for his own party? Of course not! What a day this was going to be!

True to his word, the parrot stayed away until the afternoon. He gave his feathers a special preening and polished his beak on the bark of a tree. Then he strutted back to the clearing.

It looked beautiful. There were garlands of colourful flowers stretched between the trees, and all the animals of the jungle were gathered around. In the centre, there was a big space for the guest of honour. In fact, a very big space indeed for a parrot.

As the parrot entered, a great cheer went up. The parrot tried to look modest, as all the animals broke into song together.

"Happy Birthday to you,
Happy Birthday to you,
Happy Birthday, dear ELEPHANT!
Happy Birthday to you!"

WHAT? The parrot fell off his perch as the elephant came into the clearing. It wasn't his own birthday at all!

After the elephant's party, the parrot was a changed bird. No longer did he listen to gossip or try to find out other animals' secrets. In fact, he's the kind of parrot you might not mind telling a secret to yourself nowadays – well, *almost.*

The
Reserve
Reindeer

Have you ever wondered what would happen if one of Santa Claus' reindeer couldn't pull the sleigh one Christmas? What if one of them had a pulled muscle or a bad cold? There are a lot of nasty germs about at that time of year. The answer is that there is always a reserve reindeer – a reindeer who waits patiently in his stable over Christmas in case one of the other reindeer is a little off colour.

Now being a reserve reindeer is a little like being the understudy for a leading role in a play. Although it is very good to be a part of everything, and they wouldn't want anything bad to happen to *anyone*, most understudies can't help hoping at one time or another that something will happen to the leading actor or actress. Not anything really serious, of course. Just a little bit of a sore throat, or the tiniest sprained ankle. After all, every understudy needs a chance to show the rest of the world just what he or she is made of.

Reindeer are no different. There was once a reserve reindeer who longed for the chance to fly with the other reindeer, pulling Santa's sleigh across the sky and delivering parcels to children all over the world who have been good.

"It must be wonderful," the reserve reindeer would sigh, "to give pleasure to so many little ones every year."

"It's hard work," said one reindeer, who had been in the first team for several years.

"It's dreadfully cold," said another, munching some hay.

"You've no idea how heavy that sleigh is when we set off," said a third. "And as you know, we have to return several times to fill it up again during the night."

"It's not a job for youngsters," said the fourth reindeer. "You need to be big, fit and strong for this job."

The reserve reindeer listened in silence. He was sure that everything they were saying was true, but even so, he wanted more than anything to help Santa.

But on Christmas Eve, when Santa went out to make the final check of the reindeer, every one of them seemed to be in top condition. The old man in red ran his hands along their backs and down their legs. He made sure that their antlers weren't wobbly and their noses were as cold as they should be. Then he pronounced them all fit and ready for work. There was no place for the reserve reindeer.

The reserve reindeer watched as the first team were buckled into their harnesses. Santa's elves had nimble little fingers, used to doing up each one of the complicated straps and buckles.

The sleigh was already loaded for the first time, piled high with presents for children in every city and each little country cottage.

Finally, Santa went round and had a quiet word with each of the reindeer in turn, giving them each a special piece of apple or a favourite sweet to encourage them in the difficult task ahead.

As the old man climbed into the sleigh and picked up the reins, the reserve reindeer felt the same excitement he experienced every year. Even if he was not part of the team, it was a wonderful sight to see the huge sleigh and the powerful reindeer go hurtling over the snow. Faster and faster they went until, with a *woosh!* they left the ground and flew up into the cold, starlit sky.

The reserve reindeer watched until the sleigh could no longer be seen, then he went back into his warm stable and settled down for a few hours.

Three times during the night, the sleigh returned to be filled again. Each time, the reserve reindeer went out and watched as the reindeer were given water and food to prepare them for the next stage of their great journey.

At last the final presents were loaded into the sleigh.

"Here we go on our last trip for this year!" called Santa. "Up, up and away, my brave reindeer. Just one more journey to make!"

Once again, the sleigh wooshed away over the snow, before lifting into the night sky. The little reindeer felt a little sad as he turned back towards his stable. It was almost over for another year.

But as he crossed the snowy yard to his stable, the reserve reindeer noticed something that Santa, busy as he was, had not. A small pile of presents had fallen off the sleigh and into a little pile of snow, where they had been hidden from Santa and his elves.

The reserve reindeer wandered over to the presents and looked at them. They were beautifully wrapped in gold, red and green paper. Santa had certainly meant to take them with him.

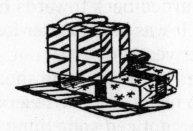

The little reindeer wondered what to do. When Santa and the reindeer returned from their last trip, it would be almost morning and far too late to make another delivery. But Santa wouldn't

want even one child to be
disappointed this Christmas.

"There's only one thing to do,"
said the little reindeer to himself.
"I'll have to deliver these
presents myself. Now where are
those elves hiding?"

The reserve reindeer knew
that he could not carry out his
plan without the help of the
elves. Quickly, he knocked on the
window of Santa's home with his
nose, so that the elves opened
the window and asked him what
he wanted. It took the reserve
reindeer no time at all to explain.

When they understood the
problem, some of the elves

looked rather guilty. It was their job, after all, to make sure that no presents were left behind. They were only too eager to help the reserve reindeer to put the mistake right. But how was he going to carry those presents? There were not very many of them, but reindeer do not have hands to carry things, and they need all four of their feet for walking or flying.

At last, one of the older elves thought of a little elf-sleigh at the back of the sleigh shed. It was quickly brought out and dusted down – just big enough for a pile of presents and one little elf.

In no time at all, the reserve reindeer found himself strapped into the sleigh. The presents were loaded, and the oldest elf stepped forward to take his seat.

"No," said the reserve reindeer. "If you don't mind, Sir, I would rather take a young elf, who is not so heavy. This is my first flight, you know."

The elves understood at once and choose a young but very sensible elf called Jingle.

"Are you ready?" called the reserve reindeer, feeling a kind of wobbly feeling in his tummy. "It's time to go. Climb on board now. It will soon be morning!"

Now the reserve reindeer had never flown even a few feet before. He knew that the magic of Christmas night would make it possible for him to fly, but even so, his heart was in his mouth as he set off across the snow at a brisk trot. Faster and faster he went, on and on. Just when he thought that he could not go any faster, he felt a strange sensation under his hooves and saw that he was several metres above the earth. He was flying!

The reserve reindeer looked back over his shoulder. "All right back there?" he called to the little elf who was clinging on behind.

"Fine!" called the excited young elf. "I think we need to swing to the left here!"

The reindeer really had no idea how to make turns in mid-air, but as soon as he *thought* about turning, he found he was doing it!

It was all going much better than the reserve reindeer had hoped, but he could feel the cold air whistling through his coat, and already his hooves were feeling tired and heavy.

"That house down there!" called the elf from the back, pointing out a small cottage with a tall chimney. To his surprise, the reindeer saw that he had flown over several towns and villages without noticing.

Carefully, the reserve reindeer began his descent. He had to time it just right so that he landed on the small roof of the cottage and didn't overshoot.

"Perfect!" called the elf, as he touched down. "The first team couldn't have done better themselves, Sir!"

The reserve reindeer felt a great burst of pride as the little elf took a present from the top of the pile and slipped it down the chimney.

"You did that well, too," smiled the reindeer. "The old man

couldn't have done it better himself either!"

For the next few hours, the reindeer and the elf were so busy that they had no time to think. By the time they had delivered the last present and turned their heads towards the North Pole, they were almost asleep.

"We must be quick," yawned the elf, "so that we can get back before the others do. I'm not sure what Santa would say if he knew we had been out on our own."

Tired as he was, the reserve reindeer put every ounce of energy he possessed into the journey home. At last he saw his

old home below him and coasted
down to land.

No sooner had the sleigh and
the reindeer touched down than
the elves came running out to
unharness him. There was
already a faint light in the
eastern sky, and on the horizon a
shape could be seen, growing
larger and larger. It was the
returning Christmas sleigh, with
Santa on board.

The elves just managed to put
the elf-sleigh away as the great
sleigh came in to land. The
reserve reindeer barely saw it
arrive. He was so tired that he
simply flopped down on to his

warm straw and was asleep before his eyes had closed.

Later that night, the little reindeer dreamed that someone dressed in red was standing over him, patting his head and putting a striped blanket over him.

"Thank you, my friend," said a voice. "You have shown the true spirit of Christmas tonight."

Then the figure disappeared, and the reindeer slept on.

I expect the little reindeer *was* dreaming, for Santa never did know about the missing presents. But on Christmas morning, the reindeer found himself covered by a very special striped blanket...

The
Foolish
Fish

Long ago, in the beautiful blue waters of the Indian Ocean, there lived a very foolish fish. The only thing he was interested in was himself and how he looked.

The fish had lovely glittering scales and flashing green fins, but still he did not believe that he was beautiful enough. Some of the other fish made fun of him.

"Have you heard the latest beauty tip from the Atlantic Ocean?" one would ask another, in the hearing of the foolish fish. "They say that if you rub seaweed into your tail every day for a month, it will grow longer and shinier. I don't know if it's true."

True or not, for the next few weeks the foolish fish could be seen rubbing his tail regularly with seaweed. At the end of the month, he was quite convinced that it looked much glossier.

"What do you think?" he asked his friend, the gubble-fish. Now gubble-fish are not well known for being clever, but they do make good friends because they try to be kind all the time.

"Your tail has always been very beautiful," said the gubble-fish. "I'm sure I don't see how it could possibly have been made lovelier. But certainly, I have never seen a tail as shiny as yours is now."

The foolish fish was very pleased, but still he wished that there was some way in which he could appear even more dashing and gorgeous.

Then, one day, the fish found a casket of jewels on the sea bed. It had come from the wreck of a sailing ship hundreds of years before, but in the clear blue waters of the ocean, the jewels sparkled as if they were new. Pearls and diamonds shone and sparkled, while emeralds, rubies and sapphires glowed green, red and blue. The jewels were in the most beautiful settings, with gold and silver chains attached.

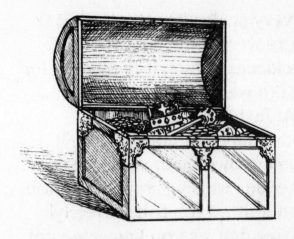

The foolish fish could not believe his eyes. Here was the answer to his prayers. If there was one thing that would make him more beautiful, it was jewellery. He looked anxiously for something that he could wear. Rubies would set off his silvery scales beautifully, but there were only brooches and necklaces, which it is difficult for fish to wear.

At last the fish spotted something absolutely right. It was a crown, with sapphires and emeralds winking around the base. And it fitted the fish perfectly!

Now fish, as you know, are not made to wear jewellery. The foolish fish found that he had to swim very, very slowly in order to stop the crown falling off. It was also quite heavy, so he found swimming hard work.

"What do you think?" he asked his fishy friends, but only the

gubble-fish had anything nice to say. The others all thought the foolish fish looked plain silly.

Now the fish loved his crown so much that he could hardly think of anything else. That is why he did not notice when all the other fish around swam quickly away one afternoon. Old man octopus was on the prowl, and it is a good idea not to come within reach of his twirly-whirly tentacles.

By the time the foolish fish noticed that the other fish had gone, it was too late. One of old man octopus's tentacles had already twisted itself around his tail, and another was wrapping itself around his silvery scales.

But as the fish wriggled in the octopus's embrace, his crown fell off into the water. The octopus, thinking it was a specially tasty snack, used two more tentacles to catch it as it drifted down and pop it into his mouth.

Have you ever seen an octopus with indigestion? It is not a pretty sight. First he went green. Then he went purple. Then he made some rather rude burping noises. At last, the pain was so bad that the octopus wrapped all of his eight tentacles around his sore tummy.

Of course, as he hugged his tummy, the octopus let go of the foolish fish, who swam away as fast as his fins would carry him.

You might think that the fish had learnt his lesson, for if the crown had not made him swim so slowly, old man octopus would never have caught him. But I'm sorry to say that he really is a very foolish fish.

"That crown saved my life!" he says to anyone who will listen.

If you see the foolish fish swimming in his new crown, you should make the most of it, for a certain eight-legged animal has a serious score to settle...

The
Invisible
Dog

One Christmas, Harry wanted one thing more than anything else. In fact, he wanted it so badly that he convinced himself he would get it for sure.

"I'm being given a dog for Christmas," he boasted to the other boys at school.

"You are not!" shouted the boys. "Your family can't afford it. Everyone knows that!"

No one liked Harry very much. He was a loner, and the other boys ignored him. Besides, he was poor and couldn't go to the cinema or the café with them.

Harry's father had been ill for a long time, and his mother could not earn very much and look after her three children as well. She knew very well what Harry wanted for Christmas, but it would be a struggle to put food on the table, never mind giving all the children expensive presents. Harry's Mum knew that there was no way her little boy's dream could come true.

But Harry was a determined little boy, and he had a strong imagination. He wasn't going to let a little thing like money stop him from having what he wanted.

When the children came back to school after Christmas, they all wanted to tell each other about the presents they had received. Harry had a smile on his face.

"Bet you didn't get a dog!" cried the other boys, but Harry only smiled.

"I did," he said. "I got the most beautiful dog you've ever seen."

"So where is it?" asked the boys with a sneer.

"You can see it tonight, if you like, when I take him for his walk," said Harry. "His name's Jack, and he's very lively."

None of the boys could believe that Harry had really been given a dog, but he seemed so certain that they began to wonder. After school, they all gathered outside Harry's house and waited for him to come out.

It was not long before Harry emerged with a rush, as though something was pulling him along. He held both his hands out in front of himself, as though he was hanging on to something for dear life. But none of the watching boys could see a dog.

"You're just pretending," they jeered. "There's no dog there!"

"Sorry," called Harry, rushing past. "I can't get him to stop! Did I mention that he's invisible?"

An invisible dog! A likely story! None of the boys believed it for a moment, but then they couldn't quite believe that Harry would pretend like this, either. Surely he must realise how silly he looked? He was much too old to have an imaginary "friend".

But Harry's belief in the dog didn't waver for a moment. Half an hour later, he returned, out of breath and muddy, looking down at his side from time to time. The dog, apparently, was walking calmly along beside him.

"I think I've tired him out," said Harry cheerfully. "See you all tomorrow! Down, Jack!"

The boys looked at each other. There wasn't a dog, was there?

Night after night, Harry left his house to take Jack for a walk.

"He's getting bigger, isn't he?" he called to the other boys. For it had become a daily habit for them to watch Harry walking his so-called invisible dog.

"One night he'll slip up," said one of the boys. "He won't come out, or he'll forget to pretend to hold the lead. Then we'll catch him out."

But Harry never forgot to hold the lead. He often bent down to pat the dog, and he talked about his Jack as proudly as any of the other boys talked about their pets. Gradually, the boys' feelings changed. They did not believe that there was a dog, but they did believe that Harry thought there was. He wasn't trying to trick them or make fun of them. He really believed that he had a dog called Jack. In a strange way, the boys began to respect the little outsider more.

One Saturday morning, the boys came across Harry running wildly down the road.

"Have you seen Jack?" he called. "Oh Jack, where are you? JACK!"

The boys could see how upset Harry was.

"Where did you see him last?" they asked.

"I took him out for a walk this morning, down to the playing field. I let him off his lead to have a run about. He started chasing birds and ran off towards the road. I haven't seen him since!" said Harry, near to tears.

"We'll help you look for him," said the boys. Then they looked at each other in confusion. How could they possibly help to find a dog they couldn't see?

But as they came round the corner towards the busy junction, Harry darted forward and knelt by the side of the road.

"Oh Jack," he sobbed, "I told you not to run out into the

traffic. Now we'll never have fun together again." And he cradled his arms around something invisible on the pavement.

"Is he…?" asked one of the boys gently.

"Yes," sobbed Harry.

"He was a wonderful dog." One of the boys put an arm around Harry's shoulder.

"I wish we could have seen him too," said another boy.

"He was the best dog ever," agreed all the others.

"Now that you don't have Jack, you'll have to play with us," suggested another boy. "But we'll never forget him, Harry."

The
Kittens
Who
Quarrelled

When Mrs Blenkinsop's cat had kittens, she intended to give them all away to good homes. The two little black and white ones found new owners very quickly, but the other two, although they were very cute and cuddly, were still at home with her after three months.

"I'm not very likely to find homes for you now," said Mrs Blenkinsop. "I suppose I shall have to keep you, although there is hardly room for three cats in my little flat."

But Mrs Blenkinsop had a little flap in her front door, so that the cat and kittens could come and go during the day, and all might have been well with her large family if only those kittens hadn't quarrelled!

It was dreadful! Night and day those two cuddly-looking kittens were arguing and fighting. If one of them wanted to play with a ball of wool, the other one wanted it. If one kitten wanted to sit on Mrs Blenkinsop's lap, the other one wanted to as well. And Mrs Blenkinsop was not a very large lady!

The kittens had a lovely basket to curl up in at night, but could they lie still until morning? Oh no! They never could agree

about which was the most
comfortable spot, so they were
up and down, wailing and
complaining, all night long.

At last Mrs Blenkinsop could
stand it no longer. "If you kittens
can't be friendly with each other,
as sisters should be, then one of
you will have to go to the cats'
home and hope that they can
find you a new place to live." she
said crossly.

Of course, the kittens were just
as quarrelsome as ever the next
day, so Mrs Blenkinsop took
action. She picked up the nearest
kitten, popped it into a basket,
and went straight down to the

cats' home as she had promised.

Mrs Blenkinsop was sorry to say goodbye to the kitten, of course, but she was a practical woman. Enough was enough.

She returned home, looking forward to a peaceful evening in front of the television.

Oh dear! She couldn't have been more wrong! All that evening the single kitten wailed and whined. She patted Mrs Blenkinsop with her paws until the poor woman was ready to scream. And she had such a pitiful, sorrowful expression on her face that it would have broken your heart to have seen it.

Mrs Blenkinsop wasn't about to have any nonsense. "You miss your sister now," she told the kitten, "but you'll soon be used to living here with your mother. After all, you don't miss your first two sisters any more, do you? Now be a good girl."

But the little kitten did not forget. Every night, she sat right outside Mrs Blenkinsop's bedroom, making a noise that sounded for all the world like a child crying.

In the morning, the little kitten wouldn't touch her breakfast – or her supper either. She simply sat and looked up at Mrs Blenkinsop with big, sad eyes.

Mrs Blenkinsop stood it for three days and three nights. Then she could bear it no longer. She put on her hat and coat and hurried off down the road.

"I just hope I'm not too late," she muttered to herself.

Mrs Blenkinsop was breathless when she reached the cats' home.

"Have you found a home for that kitten I brought in on Tuesday?" she asked anxiously.

"Impossible!" cried the man behind the desk. "No one wants a kitten that wails all the time and won't eat."

"I do," said Mrs Blenkinsop firmly, "for I have another one just the same at home."

How happy the two kittens were to be together again – for five minutes. Then the quarrelling started again. But as Mrs Blenkinsop says, "What's a little quarrelling – between friends?"

The Forgetful Elephant

Everyone knows the old saying: an elephant never forgets. Well, that's all very well in its way, but what if you are an elephant who *does* forget? It's even worse to be forgetful if the whole world expects you to be one of those famous unforgetful types.

That was the problem with Elliot the elephant. He was an excellent fellow in every way, except that he simply could not remember things from one day to the next. He tried tying knots in his tail to remind himself, but he kept forgetting to look round and see whether his tail had knots in it – or not! He even tried tying knots in his trunk, but it was so painful that he decided even forgetting things was better than *that*.

Now it wouldn't have mattered at all if Elliot had been a warthog or a hippopotamus. No one expects them to remember anything at all. When was the last time *you* asked a warthog the date of his nextdoor neighbour's birthday? You see what I mean.

Well, almost every day of his life, one animal or another came up to Elliot and said something like this: "Elliot, you're an elephant, so you'll remember this. My friend and I can't agree whether it was last year that the waterhole was muddied by those huge hippos or the year before. Can you settle the argument?"

Ninety-nine times out of a hundred, Elliot couldn't even remember that the waterhole had been muddied, never mind which year it was. He was quite hopeless, you see.

Now, you will ask why, if all the animals knew how forgetful Elliot was, they kept asking him to remember things. What a silly question! Do you know the average memory span of a giraffe or an antelope? It's about ten minutes, which is perhaps why elephants gained such a big reputation for remembering things in the first place.

Now Elliot hated letting the other animals down, but he didn't know what to do about it. Then, one day, a little bird came and perched on his ear.

"Excuse me, Elliot," he chirped, "but you and I can help each other. I hurt my wing the other year, so I can't fly very well, and I'm frightened to bits that one of these big animals – especially the huge hippos – will tread on me one day, before I have a chance to fly away. So I was wondering if I could perch on your ear like this, and in return, I will whisper *into* your ear the answers to all the questions the animals ask you. I have an excellent memory."

Elliot agreed at once, and the plan worked perfectly. Whatever question was asked, the little bird knew the answer. He then whispered it into Elliot's ear, and Elliot boomed out the reply for all to hear. *Everyone* was happy.

What? How long was the bird's memory? Oh, about ten minutes. It was just that he was clever enough to realise that if no one *else* could remember, it didn't matter *what* he said!

The
Bungle
Bird

Once upon a time, there was a bird that was so rare hardly anyone had ever seen it. Its name was the bungle bird. This rare bird was not very beautiful. It was brown and small. I did not have a gorgeous tail or a striped beak. In fact, to look at, it was very ordinary indeed. But the bungle bird had the most extraordinary song in the world. People who heard it declared it was like angels singing, and it is said that no one could ever be unkind or cruel again if they had once heard the bungle bird sing.

Now the bungle bird lived in a remote part of the world, but its lovely forest home was gradually destroyed by farmers and miners, until at last there were only two bungle birds left on the whole planet.

"If we stay here," said the male bungle bird, "there will be nowhere for us to raise little bungle birds. We must try to find a new home."

So the two bungle birds flew off across the forest, singing as they went. And the farmers and miners who heard them put down their tools and wept at the sound, for it was so beautiful. They vowed to harm the land no more, but the bungle birds did not know this, and they flew on.

Soon the bungle birds found themselves flying across the great ocean, where fishermen were scooping all the life from the sea.

"We will not find anywhere to build a nest here," said the female bird. "We must fly on until we reach dry land." And she flapped her wings harder, singing with all her heart as she went.

Far below on the stormy seas, the fishermen heard a sound that almost broke their hearts. They decided to stop plundering the sea of its creatures. But the bungle birds did not know this, and they flew on.

Before long, the bungle birds found themselves flying across a great city. As far as the eye could see there were buildings belching smoke and fumes.

"Oh, I can hardly breathe," coughed the male bungle bird. "We must fly farther still."

But in the dark smoke, the two birds lost sight of each other. Both of them sang and sang to try to tell the other where they were, but it was no use.

Far below, the people of the city heard music that made them want to dance and cry at the same time. They decided to do something about the horrible smoke that was filling the air. But it was too late for the last two bungle birds.

Some people say they are still flying and singing about the world, trying to find each other before it is too late. Others say that they died long ago, and it is only the echo of their song that can be heard drifting on the air.

If you go outside, and look and listen hard, you might be lucky enough to hear or see a bungle bird. If not, you will hear other birds and see other animals and plants that make you want to dance and cry. Don't let them call to you in vain...

The
Curious
Kitten

Some kittens like nothing better than to cuddle up to their mothers all day. They may purr a little. They may lick their fluffy coats with tiny pink tongues. But they have already decided that they will be the kind of cats who sit in front of the fire or on their owner's lap and are perfectly happy as long as their tummies are full and their paws are warm.

But there are adventurous kittens too. Almost from the moment they are born, they are trying to climb out of the basket where their mother is sitting comfortably. Over and over again, she picks them up gently by the scruff of the neck and carries them back to their warm bed. Five minutes later, they are off again, staggering across the floor before their little legs are strong enough to support them properly. They have already decided that they will be active cats, out and about at all times of the day and night.

When Carmelita Cat had her kittens, she knew almost at once that one of them was going to be more trouble than the other four put together.

He managed to fall out of the basket within hours of being

born. Even before he had opened his shiny green eyes, he was trying to explore the world around him.

The little girl who looked after Carmelita Cat was called Cassie. She spent a long time trying to think of names for the five fluffy new kittens.

"What do you think of Willow?" she asked her mother. "Like pussy willow, you know."

"That's lovely," said her mother, "but what about the other four? I think it's nice if all the names have something in common. If one of them is Willow, perhaps the others should have tree names too. What about Hazel, for example?"

Cassie decided that Hazel and Willow were quite good names for kittens, but after that she got stuck. She even looked in her encyclopedia for other tree names. Somehow, it didn't seem right to call a kitten Pine, or Ash, or Birch, or Hawthorn.

"They're not very cuddly names," she explained to her mother, "so I've had another idea. If Carmelita Cat's names begin with a "c" and my name begins with a "c", maybe the kittens' names should begin with a "c" too!"

Cassie's mother agreed that this seemed a good idea. That afternoon, she sat down with her little daughter to make a big list of names beginning with "c". It was hard at first, but then Cassie's mother remembered that she still had a book of babies' names from when she was trying to think of a name for Cassie!

After that it was much easier to decide which names were suitable for five cuddly kittens. Cassie made three lists. At the top of the first, she wrote: "I like these." At the top of the second, she wrote: "These are OK too." At the top of the third list, she wrote: "These are the wrong kinds of names for kittens." The only problem was that it was much easier to find names to put in the third list than to fill the first two lists. Cuthbert, Curzon, Cressida and Clytemnestra went into the third list straight away. So did Curtis, Colin, Cecilia and Cyril. Cleopatra, Caroline, Chloe and Catherine went into the "These are OK too." list, but after two long hours, there was still only one name in the "I like these." list.

"I like it because it's short and sweet," Cassie explained. The name was Candy.

This time it was Cassie who had a good idea. "Short and sweet!" she exclaimed. "I'll name all the kittens after my favourite sweets, whether they begin with a "c" or not!"

And before her mother had time to agree or disagree, the names just floated straight into the little girl's head.

"Candy, Fudge, Toffee and Lollipop!" she laughed. "Those are just the right kinds of names for kittens. The white one can be Candy. The two brown ones can be Fudge and Toffee. And the stripey one can be Lollipop. They're all perfect!"

"Just a minute," laughed her mother, "aren't you forgetting someone?" And she pointed at the floor, where the fifth little kitten was once again heading out across the carpet.

"He's sweet in a way," said Cassie doubtfully, "but not in a fluffy, cuddly kind of way. I can't imagine calling *him* a sugary name, can you?"

"Well, no," her mother agreed, "but I do think he looks as though he could be called Peanut, and that's a snack, if not a sweet."

"Peanut is fine," agreed Cassie. And she bent down to give

Candy, Fudge, Toffee, Lollipop *and* Peanut a big hug.

Do you know someone who is never ever called by his or her real name? Often no one can remember quite why that is. You know, that's exactly what happened to the adventurous kitten. After that first day of being called Peanut, he never heard the name again. And that was because it soon became obvious that there was only one name that really suited his character. From that day to this, he has been called Pickle. And from that day to this, he has *been* in a pickle almost *all* the time.

As soon as his eyes were open, the naughty little kitten set off to explore the world. He soon found the door to the kitchen and all the delicious things that were inside. When *all* the cakes for some visitors' tea were found to have tiny little bites in them, it didn't take long to follow a trail of crumbs back to the cushion were Pickle was taking a nap. You never saw such an innocent little sleeping face!

To tell you the truth, Pickle felt a little bit ill after so many sweet mouthfuls. When he felt better, he decided to explore the rest of the house. In the bathroom, he found that he could nudge one of the taps with his paw and get a nice drink of cool water. Unfortunately, it didn't occur to the curious kitten to nudge the tap *back* again, so Cassie's father slipped straight into a large puddle on the floor when he came in to brush his teeth. He blamed Cassie first and then her mother, until his wife pointed out that *he* had been in the bathroom last. Luckily for Pickle,

his wet pawprints had dried as
the tap dripped.

The next day, Pickle decided to
see what was in the bedrooms.
He pulled seventeen socks out
from underneath Cassie's
brother's bed, much to the
amazement of everyone in the
house who had ever lost a sock.

"I don't *know* how they got
there," wailed Cassie's brother.

In Cassie's parents' room,
Pickle discovered that he could
climb up the chest of drawers
and perch on top of the
wardrobe. It was rather an effort
to make the climb, so when he
got to the top, he had a little rest.

When he woke up, several hours later, it was completely dark. Pickle was a clever little kitten and he thought he could remember which side the bed was on. Bravely, he jumped out into the blackness.

"Oooowwww! Help! We're being attacked! There are dozens of them! Help!"

Cassie's dad had been rudely awakened by a kitten in the middle of his tummy, just as he was dreaming of capturing a gang of criminals single-handed. Cassie's mother, who didn't know *what* was going on, was halfway through dialling the

number of the police station
before she realised that she
could hear the patter of tiny feet
scampering down the hallway.

"It was that wretched kitten!"
she whispered. "Ssshh! You'll
wake the children. You wouldn't
want *them* to know that you'd
been attacked by a kitten, would
you, dear?"

Cassie's dad said some rather
rude words and went back to
sleep, but not before he had
searched under the bed and over
the wardrobe and shut the door
very firmly indeed.

Meanwhile, Pickle was being
told off by Carmelita Cat in no

uncertain terms. She was really worried about her little one.

"If you go on like this, my son," she said, "you will be turned out into the garden and only let in twice a day for meals. That happens to some cats, you know."

But Pickle thought that sounded quite an interesting idea. He had always wondered about the world outside the house, and now he knew that some cats lived in it. The very next day, he decided to explore the garden.

The garden of the house where Cassie lived was not, in fact, very big. There was a patch of grass with rather a lot of weeds in it, a few bushes, and a path leading to a gate at the end.

It didn't take Pickle long to discover that there was nothing very interesting in the garden, but it did seem as though there were places worth visiting outside the garden. With no thought of danger or of getting lost, the kitten jumped over the gate and set off into the countryside.

It was a beautifully warm and sunny day when the little kitten set out. In no time at all, he had seen a lifetime's number of wonderful things. There was a butterfly sunning its wings on a huge pink flower. There was a line of hundreds of tiny ants marching across the path. Pickle had his nose bitten several times and learned not to tickle ants with his whiskers.

Further along the path, there was a little pond with a duck swimming happily on it. Pickle dipped his paw into the water and was delighted to see large ripples fanning out into the middle of the pond. The duck, being twice as big as the kitten, quacked crossly at him for disturbing the fish. Pickle, of course, was too small to understand more than a few words of foreign languages, so he simply miaowed at the duck and wandered on, although he did think that he had understood the word "fish", and this made him feel extremely hungry.

You must remember that Pickle was only a very young kitten. His mother had not had time to teach him everything he should know. So when Pickle felt peckish, the only thing he could think of doing was going back to the house and diving into one of the six little bowls of cat food that sat on a special mat in the hall. In fact, now that he came to think of it, he was so hungry that he might dive into more than one of the bowls, he thought.

As soon as Pickle turned back to find his way home, he realised that he had a very big problem. He couldn't for the life of him remember whether he had to turn left or right at the pond. Things looked different, somehow, from the opposite direction. He knew that the path went straight on past the butterfly, but when he saw, with a sinking feeling in his tummy, that butterflies can fly from flower to flower, he had to admit that he was well and truly lost. He might never see Candy and Fudge and Toffee and Lollipop and his big, cuddly mother again!

Now Pickle, as we know, was a brave little cat, and he sat down by the path to try to work out what to do. As he did so, he noticed one of the butterflies flitting up, up, up into a tree high above him.

"From up there," Pickle said to himself, "I'll be able to see farther even than from the top of the wardrobe. Perhaps I'll be able to see my way home."

This, of course, was not such a bad idea, but Pickle had never climbed anything as high as a tree before. Luckily, there was a ladder leaning against the tree, just right for little paws to climb.

When he reached the first pair of branches, Pickle had a rest. He knew that he would have to climb much higher if he was going to see all the way back to the tiny garden and the cosy house. It was tempting to rest for a long time in the sunshine, but Pickle remembered what had happened the last time he had fallen asleep

in a high place. When he woke up in the bedroom, it had been dark. The last thing that Pickle wanted now was to be lost *and* alone in the dark in a strange place. He was brave, but not *that* brave!

So the little kitten climbed on to the very top of the tree. He could see for miles in every direction. And sure enough, that tiny house far below was his home. He even thought that he could see Cassie lying on the little patch of grass with her book. From up here, she looked as tiny as one of the marching ants he had seen earlier. Now it would be easy to get home.

I don't know if you have ever climbed a tree yourself, but you may know that climbing *up* a tree is a very different matter from climbing *down* a tree. Somehow, all the branches that seemed so strong and safe on the way up seemed to sway alarmingly now. It didn't help that a breeze had begun to blow. Clouds blew across the sun and the leaves, which had glistened in the sunshine, now began to shake and whisper among themselves. Pickle almost thought he could hear them saying, "He won't get down, oh no, oh no. He won't get down, oh no."

Finally, the brave little kitten could go no further. He sat on a branch, high above the ladder, and began to miaow sadly to himself. He was afraid that his life of adventure might be over almost before it had begun.

Meanwhile, back at the house, Cassie had noticed that one of the six little bowls she had filled earlier was still full. She went into the sitting room and peered into Carmelita's basket. There was the mother cat, purring proudly, and cuddled around her were four little kittens. Cassie counted them one by one: Candy, Fudge, Toffee and Lollipop. Where was Pickle?

Cassie hunted all over the house. She was specially careful to look under her brother's bed and on top of her parents' wardrobe. There was no little kitten to be seen. The little girl went out into the garden and called him.

"Pickle! Pickle! Where are you?" There was no reply.

All that afternoon, Cassie searched, but as the sun began to sink in the sky, she still had not found the missing kitten.

"He's lost for ever," she sobbed to her mother.

"You know," her mother replied with a smile, "mothers are very good at looking after their children. Why don't you ask Carmelita Cat to help you?"

Cassie whispered her problem in the mother cat's furry ear. Carmelita gave a big sigh and a huge stretch. Then she climbed over her sleeping kittens and trotted out of the back door and into the garden, with Cassie following anxiously behind.

Down the path went Carmelita, her tail held high, and down the path went Cassie, not at all sure that her mother's plan was going to work.

At the end of the garden, Carmelita Cat waited for Cassie

to open the gate. She decided that it wouldn't be dignified to jump over it at her age. Through the gate, the wise cat trotted on, down the grassy path and past the little pond. The dabbling duck knew better than to quack at a cat on a mission, and he ducked his head under the water.

A little way further on, Cassie saw a tree with a ladder leaning against it. Better still, she heard a plaintive little miaow coming from its branches.

"Oh, Pickle!" cried Cassie. "Your mother has come for you."

But Carmelita Cat didn't climb the tree. Oh no. She sat at the bottom and gave three sharp miaows, which meant something rather cross in cat language. Pickle suddenly found that he might just be able to get down after all...

When Pickle was safely back at home that night, Cassie made him promise that he would *never* go exploring without her again. But the little kitten *still* wasn't very good at foreign languages, so I'm not at all sure he understood. What do *you* think?

A Kitten
for
Christmas

Everyone likes to receive gifts, especially at Christmas, but even the nicest present can seem disappointing if you have set your heart on something else.

That is just what happened to Ashley one Christmas not so long ago. Weeks before the big day, she began making her list for Father Christmas.

"He's a very busy man," she told her older sister. "I'm going to make sure he gets my list before anyone else's, so he has time to find the things I want."

"You'll be lucky," muttered her sister, whose name was Eleanor. "I tried that years ago and I still

didn't get the bike I wanted …
well, not until I was eight, anyway."

"I don't want a bike," Ashley
retorted. "I'm going to ask for
something much better than that."

"What?" asked Eleanor, putting
down her book.

"I can't tell you," said Ashley.

"Yes, you can," said Eleanor.
"I won't tell anyone *and* I can
help you to spell it, so Father
Christmas won't make a mistake."

"No," said Ashley firmly. "If I
tell you, it won't come true. It's
a secret. Father Christmas will
know what I mean however I
spell it, and anyway, I'm going to
draw him a picture as well."

"Well, don't blame me if it all goes *horribly* wrong," giggled Eleanor. "Little girls don't always get what they want, you know."

"They do," said Ashley, "it they want it badly enough. Everyone knows that." She took her piece of paper and went off to her secret place to finish the list and draw a very special picture. Because the thing she wanted mustn't be just any old kind. She knew exactly how it should look.

When she had finished her list, Ashley took it over to her granny's house so that she could put it on the fire and watch it whirl up the chimney. Her granny told her that was how to make sure that Father Christmas saw her list as quickly as possible.

"It will fly through the air to the North Pole," explained Granny, "and get there much quicker than ordinary post, which has to go across the sea and ice."

Ashley was a little worried that Father Christmas would deliver her present to her granny's house if she sent her list up her granny's chimney, but Granny said he would understand that Ashley's house had central heating and there weren't any chimneys for the message to fly up. As Granny was usually right, Ashley did just as she said, and as the list turned to ashes and floated up the chimney, she shut her eyes tight and made the biggest wish she had ever wished.

After that, it didn't occur to Ashley for one minute that her dream might not come true. She knew she had wished with all her heart and she trusted her granny and Father Christmas. As Christmas grew nearer, Ashley became more and more excited.

"It won't be long now," she told Eleanor. "I don't know how I'll be able to sleep on Christmas Eve, I'll be so excited. But I wouldn't want to do anything to keep Father

Christmas away. He's quite shy, you know. That's why children don't often see him."

"Don't count your chickens before they're hatched," said Eleanor grandly, which didn't make much sense to Ashley.

"I didn't ask for chickens!" she said. "That would be silly."

"What did you ask for?" asked Eleanor. "You can tell me now."

Ashley was so excited that she wanted to tell very badly. But she held her lips tightly together and screwed up her face. She looked so funny that her mother asked her if she had a toothache when she saw her strange expression.

Well, Ashley didn't sleep very well on Christmas Eve, but she didn't dare to open her eyes in case she caught sight of a shy old man in a red coat. Towards dawn, she couldn't stay awake any longer, so she didn't hear the rustling and bustling at the foot of her bed just as the sun was rising.

Christmas Day dawned bright and clear. There wasn't any snow, which was rather disappointing, but everything else was perfect. There were lots of exciting-looking presents at the bottom of Ashley's bed, which she carefully carried into the sitting room, so that everyone could watch her as she unwrapped them. The special present she was expecting didn't seem to be there, but then she wasn't really expecting it.

"After all," she said to herself, "it would need to be wrapped up very, very carefully."

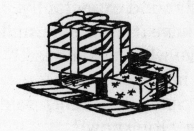

It took ages for everyone to open their presents. Ashley had some really nice things, such as a watch from her parents and a big book of fairy stories from her granny, but she was so excited about the other present she knew must be waiting that she hardly paid attention to all the other lovely things.

When everyone had finished all their unwrapping, Ashley looked round expectantly.

"I'll have it now," she smiled.

"Have what, sweetheart?" asked her father.

"My Special Present," said Ashley. "*You* know!"

"No, I don't," her father laughed. "You've had all your presents now. Don't you like them?"

"Yes." Ashley was impatient now. "But my main present is

still to come, isn't it? You can
bring it out now, can't you?"

"Really, there isn't anything else,
Ashley," said her mother. "I hope
you're not being a greedy girl."

Ashley thought they were joking
at first, but when she looked up
into their faces, she could see that
her parents were telling the truth.
Her special present was not
going to come. Ashley couldn't
help it, even on Christmas Day.
She burst into tears.

"She's over-excited," said her
mother. "And she probably didn't
get much sleep either. What is it,
darling? What was it that you
wanted so badly?"

"C-c-can I say it now?" Ashley asked Eleanor, tears running down her cheeks.

"Yes, of course you can," said Eleanor. "I told you it might not come, you know."

"What might not come?" asked Ashley's mother gently. "What was it, my love?"

"My k-k-kitten," sobbed Ashley. "I was going to call her Holly, because it's Christmas."

Ashley's father laughed. "I'm not having a cat in this house," he said, "and that's final. It will sharpen its claws on the furniture and leave mice in my slippers. No, thank you. No cats here!"

Ashley couldn't believe her ears, but her father was serious.

"I really don't like cats very much," he explained. "There will be hairs on all the furniture and smelly food in the kitchen. There's no question, sweetheart, of your having a kitten. I don't know what gave you that idea."

Poor Ashley! She tried very hard to hide her disappointment and enjoy the rest of Christmas, but it was very hard. She could not forget that by now she should have been cuddling a little friend called Holly. Even when snow began to fall in the afternoon, she could not feel more cheerful.

By teatime, the snow was lying thick on the ground and darkness was beginning to fall. Ashley tried hard to smile as she ate her mince pie. Her father, seeing how unhappy she was, gave her a specially large piece of cake, but Ashley simply pushed it around her plate.

"I think it's been a tiring day for little ones," said her mother, "and we should all have an early night. We'll feel better tomorrow."

Ashley obediently had her bath and went to bed. She really *was* very tired, and her little bed felt warm and comforting.

"I won't forget you, Holly,"

Ashley whispered into her pillow. When she shut her eyes to go to sleep, she could almost see a little white kitten gazing up at her.

Ashley began to slip into the land of dreams. As she did so, she heard a miaowing sound close by. It seemed too real to be part of a dream, but surely there couldn't truly be a kitten nearby?

The miaowing sounded pitiful in the cold night air. Ashley could bear it no longer. She crawled down to the end of her bed and looked out of the window. She felt sure that the miaowing was coming from the garden. Could it be real after all?

Ashley didn't know what to do. Usually, she would have woken her father and mother and told them what she had heard, but she thought that her father might be cross if she mentioned the subject of kittens again.

"I'll have to go and look myself," she said to herself, pulling on her coat to keep herself warm.

But Ashley need not have worried about her father. He too had heard the heartrending sound and he could not bear the idea of an animal in trouble on such a cold night. He met his little daughter on the landing and took her gently by the hand.

"Let's go and have a look downstairs, sweetheart," he said. "It sounds as though someone needs our help."

Ashley and her father crept down the stairs and into the front hallway.

"Put on your boots, darling," said Ashley's father. "It is bitterly cold tonight and we may need to search in the garden. Here's my torch, and we can put the outside light on as well. Are you ready?"

Ashley nodded. She stood on tiptoe to help her father open the front door. As it swung open, snow fell from the Christmas wreath hanging outside.

But Ashley didn't need her boots and her father didn't need his torch. Their midnight visitor was sitting right on the step outside the door, her little pawprints leading away into the snow. It was the sweetest little white kitten you have ever seen.

No one could resist the appeal of the big trusting eyes looking up at them both. Ashley's father bent down and gently picked up the little cat.

"I think you'd better come inside out of the cold, little one," he said. "There's someone here who will take care of you tonight until we can find where you really belong."

Ashley certainly did take good care of the little kitten that night. She gave her some milk and a little bit of minced meat. Then she made her a cosy bed in an old cardboard box and put it at the end of her bed, so that she could hear if the little kitten woke up in the night.

That night, Ashley slept well, a happy girl again. When she woke up in the morning, she found the little white kitten asleep on her pillow, as warm and soft as the kitten she had imagined.

"I'm going to call you Holly anyway," she whispered to the kitten, "even if you do have to go back where you belong. Thank you for coming to visit us."

Ashley got dressed and carefully carried the kitten downstairs. She made it some breakfast before she had anything herself. Her mother watched with a smile and saw that her little daughter was glowing with happiness.

As Ashley sat down for her breakfast at last, and the little kitten began lapping at her milk with her pink tongue, Ashley's father put down the telephone.

"I've called everyone I can think of," he said, "and no one has any report of a missing kitten. It looks as thought this little one will be looking for a new home."

Ashley didn't dare to look up. She couldn't bear to hope that the kitten might be able to stay. Then she saw her father glance at her mother and bend down to stroke the cuddly visitor.

"It's all right, Ashley," he said. "Choosing a kitten is not something to be taken lightly, and there are lots of reasons not to do it. But when a kitten chooses *you*, that's a different matter. This little one can stay with us."

Ashley shut her eyes tight. "Thank you, Father Christmas," she whispered. "I *knew* you'd get my message."

The
Tiniest
Kitten

All kittens are tiny when they are first born, but some are smaller than others. When Farmer Brown looked down at the four little kittens curled up with their mother in his warm barn, he shook his head.

"I don't give much for that one's chances," he said. "The others will probably push him out of the way when it's time to feed, and he won't get the warmest spot next to his mum either. It sometimes happens like that, I'm afraid."

"But couldn't we take him inside and rear him ourselves?" asked his wife, who hated to see any small creature suffer and was always rescuing waifs and strays from around the farm.

"With the two lambs and the owl with a broken wing and the duck who can't swim?" asked her husband. "No, my dear, I think we must let Nature take its course. The little one may surprise us, after all."

Reluctantly, the farmer's wife left the kittens in the barn, but she couldn't get the tiniest kitten's little face out of her mind. She knew that the barn was safe from foxes and the cold spring winds, but she couldn't bear the thought of a tiny kitten being pushed out of the way by his own brothers and sisters. If that was Nature, well, it didn't seem natural somehow.

That night, the kind woman tossed and turned in her bed, while the farmer snored peacefully. Finally, she could stand it no longer. She pulled on her dressing gown and her sensible slippers and hurried downstairs.

Outside, the wind had dropped, but tiny crystals of ice were forming on everything in the farm-yard. Even cobwebs stretched across the window of the old hen shed were sparkling with frost.

The latch of the barn door was freezing to the touch, as the farmer's wife pushed it firmly down. It was always stiff, and tonight she had to use both hands to press it before she heard the click on the other side.

Inside, the barn was dark but not cold. Some chickens were roosting on the bales of straw by the doorway, but they did not stir as she switched on the one dim light that swung from high up in the rafters.

Gathering her dressing gown up in one hand, the farmer's wife climbed up the ladder to the hay loft at one end of the barn. She held her breath as she looked down at the little kittens, hoping with all her kind heart that she had not come too late.

There was the mother cat, sleeping peacefully, and there were the three healthy kittens, cuddling up to her. As she watched, one of them stretched out a tiny paw and nestled closer to his warm, furry mother.

There was no sign of the tiniest kitten.

The farmer's wife searched all over the hay loft. Three big feathery chickens clucked in protest as she moved past them. And then she heard the tiniest little sound.

The farmer's wife peered closer at the chickens. To her amazement, she saw a tiny furry body curled up underneath them. And when she stooped down to pick it up, the little kitten was still warm and quite definitely alive!

"You are the cleverest little cat I have ever seen," whispered the farmer's wife, "and you deserve to do well, even if you *are* tiny. I'm going to take you inside and hide you in my shopping basket in the warm kitchen. Only you must promise not to make a noise. And when you are bigger and stronger, you can come back in here to be with your brothers and sisters. What do you think about that?"

The little kitten, of course, didn't make a sound. He was happily dreaming of milk and cuddles and mothers who, strangely enough, clucked instead of purring.

For the next two weeks, the farmer's wife fed the little cat with warm milk little by little. Gradually, the kitten became stronger, but he hardly seemed to grow at all.

Soon the day came when the kitten was not content to lie curled up in a basket all day, under the kitchen table. He wanted to be out and about, exploring the exciting sounds and smells coming from the kitchen around the table. The farmer's wife knew what her husband would say: "If he's strong enough to explore, he can go back into the barn." She knew that the little cat could not stay in the house for ever, so one fine day, she carried him across the yard and into the warm barn. His brothers and sisters were playing in the straw, and the eager little kitten ran straight off to join them.

The farmer's wife hurried away with a smile on her face. She did not see the way that the larger kittens hissed at their brother and pushed him away when he tried to join in their games. They were not really being unkind. They were so tiny themselves when he was taken away that they did not recognise him as their brother.

Back in the farmhouse, the farmer came in for his morning coffee. He nudged the basket under the table with his toe, as he had been doing for the past two weeks. Now, for the first time, it felt light and empty.

"That kitten has gone back to the barn then," he grinned, peering at his wife over the paper. "Did you think I wouldn't notice? I hope it will be fine, love, but I'm very much afraid that the others will reject it even more now, despite your hard work to make him big and strong."

"I may have made him strong," laughed his wife, "but he never did get very big. Fancy you knowing about it all the time."

"I know *you*, my dear," smiled the farmer. "I just hope all your efforts were worth it."

The farmer put down his paper and his mug and went back outside. Before he returned to his work, he crept over to the barn and peeped inside, turning on the light for a better view.

Just as he suspected, the tiniest kitten was curled up by himself, while his brothers and sisters slept with their mother on another bale of straw.

The farmer shook his head and went back out to his tractor. He set off for some distant fields, forgetting that he had left the light on in the barn.

At first all was well in the barn, but a piece of wiring near the straw at the back had recently been gnawed by a family of hungry mice. It began to get very hot. Within a few minutes, the straw around it was smouldering gently. It took only a few minutes more for the whole pile of bales to be blazing furiously.

As soon as they realised that the barn was filling with heat and smoke, the hens and the cat began a terrible din of clucking and miaowing. They could not escape from the barn, but they scurried as fast as they could to the corner farthest from the fire.

Of course, with all the dry straw and wood in the barn, the fire spread at an alarming rate. Flames licked the walls, and smoke billowed out to fill the hay loft and curl up to the rafters high above. There was a smell of burning, and the temperature inside the barn rose and rose.

There was only one place where fresh air could get into the barn. Below the door there was quite a wide gap. Soon the cats and the hens were all crouching against the door. The gap was far too small for them to get through, but they gratefully gulped the fresh, sweet air from outside.

Now when I said that the gap was too small for the hens and the cats, that was not quite right. One little kitten *was* small enough to squeeze through. It was an effort, and he rather bruised his ears as he inched his way into the yard, but at last he stood on the other side, breathing deeply and shaking with relief at his escape.

No one knows if the tiniest kitten deliberately worked out what to do next. Perhaps he simply ran to the last place he had felt safe and cared for. Whatever the reason, he ran to the farmhouse, jumped up to the kitchen window, and scratched on it with his tiny claws, trying to get in through the glass.

Luckily, the farmer's wife had just finished her work and was gathering her things together in the kitchen, ready to go into town to deliver some eggs. She heard the tiny scratching on the window and hurried to open it.

There sat the little kitten, shivering with fright.

"You poor little mite," said the farmer's wife, cuddling him in her arms. "Have those other cats been horrid to you? Just a minute, little one, you smell of smoke!"

The worried woman looked out of the window. Sure enough, a thin plume of smoke was drifting out from under the barn door.

After that, everything happened very quickly. The farmer's wife called the fire brigade and ran to rescue the other animals in the barn. Before the farmer returned from his fields, the fire was out and twelve hens and five cats were all sheltering in the kitchen!

The farmer came back to find three large firemen having tea, surrounded by more animals than he had ever seen in his house in his life, which was really saying something!

"What on earth has been happening here?" he demanded.

It didn't take long for the farmer's wife to explain the whole dramatic story.

"The straw is all burned, I'm afraid," she said, "but thank goodness the barn is safe. And do you know who we have to thank for that? I might have gone off to do my shopping without noticing a thing if it hadn't been for this little chap." She cuddled the tiniest kitten. "And if the barn had gone up in flames, the farmhouse might not have been far behind."

"I suppose that means," said the farmer with a smile, "that we shall be having a new lodger in the basket under the table. And I won't mind at all, so long as he doesn't start nibbling my toes!"

I would like to be able to report that the other cats were grateful to the tiniest kitten for saving their lives, but they still chased him away. Luckily, he was as happy as any kitten could be in the farmhouse with his new family.

The
Christmas
Miracle

Outside, the night was cold, but the stable was full of warm straw and sleeping animals. It was the cosiest place for miles around. When two travellers stumbled into the building and curled up on the straw, the animals were not unduly surprised. They willingly shifted so there was room for the little donkey the travellers had brought with them.

"Have you come far?" the ox whispered, so that the human travellers could not hear.

"Yes," replied the donkey. "It has been a long, hard journey. And when we arrived, there was nowhere for us to stay."

Soon there was no sound in the little stable, as the animals and the human visitors all slept soundly in the still night.

But around midnight, there were quiet sounds from the corner where the humans had settled. The animals were woken by a sound they had never heard before. It was the cry of a baby, born that night in the poor stable.

The ox looked at the woman holding the baby. She seemed to be surrounded by a golden glow as she rocked the tiny child.

"She could put him in the manger that has our hay in it," the cow whispered to the donkey.

As if she had heard him, the lady put her baby carefully in the manger, where he lay quietly.

The animals did not want to frighten the little child, so they knelt gently down around him.

At first the donkey could not understand why it was so hard to go back to sleep. Then he realised that the stable was full of light. Through the cracks in the roof, starlight was streaming from one big star hovering above.

It is said that if you go into any stable at midnight on Christmas Eve, you will see the animals kneeling in memory of that special night so many years ago.